# A Way in the Wilderness

## Essays in Messianic Jewish Thought

Edited by M.G. Einspruch

Lederer Publications
Baltimore, Maryland

First edition 1981. Second edition 1989.

Printed in the United States of America

Library of Congress Catalog Card Number: 81-82106

# ACKNOWLEDGMENTS

**A Case of Mistaken Identity** reprinted by permission of Rachmiel Frydland.

**Blessed be Egypt?** by Daniel Fuchs. Reprinted from THE CHOSEN PEOPLE, February 1978. Published by The American Board of Missions to the Jews, Inc.

**By Faith** reprinted by permission of Moishe Rosen.

**Doubly Blest** reprinted by permission of Sheldon Scher.

**Good News from the Tenach** reprinted from GOOD NEWS FROM THE OLD TESTAMENT by permission of Lilli Wolff.

**Immortality in Jewish Thought** by Victor Buksbazen. Reprinted by permission.

**Is the New Testament Anti-Semitic?** by Victor Buksbazen. Reprinted by permission.

**Jesus was not a Christian** reprinted by permission of John Murray Smoot and Jews for Jesus.

**The Bible—An Historical Document** reprinted by permission of William Katin.

**The New Covenant** by J. H. Hunting, reprinted by permission of THE VINEYARD.

**Trinity is Jewish** reprinted by permission of Rachmiel Frydland.

**What is a Jew?** by S. Ostrovsky of Israel. Reprinted by permission of the author.

**Illustrations:**

*Cover* by Steffi Rubin from art of Muriel Anne Einspruch

Words with an asterisk (*) are listed in glossary.
Verses from the TENACH follow arrangement in Hebrew Bible.

# CONTENTS

# Introduction

"Behold, I will do a new thing;
Now shall it spring forth; shall ye
not know it?
I will even make **a way in the wilderness,**
And rivers in the desert.
The beasts of the field shall honor Me,
The jackals and the ostriches;
Because I give waters in the wilderness,
And rivers in the desert,
To give drink to My people, Mine elect;
The people which I formed for Myself,
That they might tell of My praise."

*Isaiah 43:19-21*

# I.E.S. —י״עס

By HENRY EINSPRUCH

Hebrew is today the official language of the State of Israel. To be sure, in Jerusalem and Tel Aviv, in Jaffa and in Safed, one can hear other tongues such as Russian, English, Bulgarian, French, Arabic, Yiddish, but Hebrew alone enjoys official status.

The revival of Hebrew as a spoken language owes much to such men as Eliezer Ben-Yehudah, J. L. Gordon, Moses Loeb Lilienblum, Abraham Mapu, Ahad Ha-Am, Perez Smolenskin, who labored assiduously to bring about the rebirth of the national tongue.

In my youth I remember coming across a copy of Shakespeare's drama *Othello*, rendered into Hebrew by I. E. S. It was my first introduction to the classics. Perez Smolenskin, the editor of *Ha-Shahar,* wrote a lengthy introduction to the book in which he spoke gleefully of the revenge we Jews have had on the English. "They took our Bible and make it their own," he went on to say, "and we, in turn, have taken their Shakespeare and brought him into the treasury of our holy language."

Years later I learned that I. E. S. was none other than Isaac Edward Salkinson, who had also translated *Romeo and Juliet*, and Milton's *Paradise Lost*.

Two men who greatly encouraged him to translate Milton's epic were Dr. C. D. Ginsburg, perhaps best known for his great work on the Masorah,* and Dr. Adolf Jellinek, the scholarly Austrian Rabbi. It was Rabbi Jellinek who suggested that the Hebrew title be *Vayegorash es Haadam* (So He Drove Out the Man).

In *The Renascence of Hebrew Literature*, page 245, Nahum Slouschz said, "It was a sign of the times that this work, wholly Christian in character, was enjoyed and appreciated by the educated Hebrew public in due accordance of its literacy merits."

Isaac Edward Salkinson was born in Wilna of strictly Orthodox parents who entertained the hope that their precocious son would some day become a rabbi. He studied in the foremost rabbinical schools of the Old World, and knew Talmud,* Bible, Jewish philosophy, and was an accomplished Hebraist.

In early manhood he went to England and settled in London in order to further his studies. One day, in an old bookstore, he came upon a copy of the New Testament in Hebrew. Until then he thought he knew every important Hebrew book, but this was something he had never even heard of. Prompted by curiosity he began to read, but curiosity soon turned to real interest.

After carefully studying and weighing the evidence, he became convinced that Jesus of Nazareth fulfilled the hopes and aspirations of the prophets, and that he was truly the Messiah of Israel.

The Hebrew New Testament which he read was a rather crude translation, and aroused in him a desire to render that sacred work into idiomatic Hebrew. He began with Paul's epistle to the *Romans*. "It was my first attempt in the work of translation," he wrote. "However, I found that to acquire the art of translation properly requires long and tedious practice. The Jews in every generation have produced great Hebrew writers, but seldom any great translators."

For nearly thirty years he labored in Vienna, where he sought to spread the Messianic idea by means of his writings and lectures, and his name became a household word in cultured Jewish circles.

When Dr. Ginsburg's monumental work on the Masorah* was going through the press in Vienna, he engaged Mr. Salkinson to read proof for him. About that time Salkinson's translation of the New Testament was nearing completion. Writing to a friend concerning his *magnum opus,* he said, "My Hebrew version of the New Testament is now ready for publication. Hebrew translation seems to be the only talent given to me, and I have consecrated it to the Lord. It is my alabaster box of precious ointment which I pour out in honor of my Saviour, that the fragrance of his name may fill the whole house of Israel."

Salkinson, however, did not live to see his cherished work in print. On the 5th of June, 1883, death overtook him, and it was his friend, Dr. C. D. Ginsburg, who undertook to do for Salkinson's work what Salkinson had done for him.

In *By-Paths in Hebraic Bookland"* (published by the Jewish Publication Society of America ), Prof. Israel Abrahams, reader of Rabbinics at Cambridge University, makes this striking observation: "Salkinson's merit lay in his power to take a work of art, pass it through the crucible of translation, and then bring out the result as a work of art still . . . I do not know whom I would place above Salkinson in the list of the best translators into Hebrew."

Modern Hebrew owes much to I. E. S., the great Messianic Jew.

# THE BIBLE ~ AN HISTORICAL DOCUMENT

By WILLIAM KATIN

It has often been alleged that the *Genesis* accounts of the career of Abraham and his descendants are untrustworthy. Perhaps many have scoffed at its accounts of ancient history.

The TENACH* records that Abraham's native city in Southern Babylonia was called Ur. The city of Ur was thoroughly excavated by Leonard Woolley (1922-34), and it proved to be a large flourishing city which enjoyed an advanced civilization around 2,000 B.C.E., which would have been precisely Abraham's period. Hence we can affirm that Abraham's origins in Ur are trustworthy.

In *Genesis* chapter 13 Abraham and Lot traveled from Egypt to the Negev. However, their herds were so great that they separated. The TENACH* records that Lot settled in the cities of the Jordan Valley. Older scholars had criticized *Genesis* 13 as unhistorical on the grounds that the Jordan Valley was relatively uninhabited in Abraham's time. But Nelson Glueck uncovered more than seventy sites in the Jordan Valley, some of them as ancient as 3,000 B.C.E.

The TENACH* avers that Isaac's wife Rebekah was raised in the city of Nahor, the city being named after Abraham's brother. The Mari Tablets were discovered by Parrot in 1933. These 20,000 tablets were written in Akkadian during the 18th century B.C.E., and confirm the existence of Nakhur (the city named after Abraham's brother).

The Mari Tablets also mention a tribe of fierce nomads by the name of Banu-Yamina. Note the similarity to the Benjamin, one of the twelve tribes of Israel.

*Genesis* chapter 12 records God's promise of a son to Abraham. Abraham's lack of faith is noted in *Genesis* 15 where Eliezer is presented as Abraham's adopted son. Abraham had not waited for the promised son Isaac. Once again archaeology illustrated the historicity of a biblical account. God's rejection of Abraham's "adoption" of Eliezer might have embarrased Abraham. However, the Nuzi Tablets of the 15th century B.C.E. note the custom for the claims of an adopted son to be set aside if a natural heir was subsequently born into the family.

*Genesis* chapter 25 registers the account of Esau coming home from the field and savoring Jacob's stew. Jacob would not give Esau some stew unless Esau would first sell him the birthright. This was a large demand as the birthright included the leadership of the tribe and the bulk of the family property. The Nuzi Tablets attest this custom and so affirm the historicity of this account.

As Isaac lay upon his deathbed, as accounted in *Genesis* chapter 27, Jacob tricked his father into giving him the blessing. Later, when Esau came before his father's deathbed, Isaac realized that he had been tricked. However, the deathbed promise could not be rescinded. This binding character of a deathbed will is also attested in Nuzi.

Laban's deception in *Genesis* chapter 29 gave Jacob a taste of his own medicine. As Jacob was about to leave his father-in-law, Rachel tried to financially protect her husband. Therefore Rachel stole the household gods. The Nuzi Tablets record the case of a man able to claim the estate of his father-in-law because he possessed the family household gods. Archaeology once again supports the reliability of the biblical account.

This is a small portion of the available material which shows the historicity of the TENACH.* Now let us briefly examine the New Testament to see if it can be classified as an historical document.

Often the New Testament is viewed as equivalent to the written conclusion of a modern party game of "telephone." Some scholars have decreed that Jesus' original words and deeds have been so obscured by later followers that it is difficult, if not impossible, to view the New Testament as an historical document.

There are in existence about 4,000 Greek manuscripts of the New Testament. One example is the Chester Beatty Biblical Papyri, the existence of which was made public in 1931. It consists of portions of eleven papyrus codices, three of which contained most of the New Testament dating from 200 C.E.

Perhaps we can appreciate how wealthy the New Testament is in manuscript attestation if we compare the textual material for other ancient historical works. For Caesar's *Gallic War* (composed between 58-50 B.C.E.) there are several existing manuscripts, but only nine or ten are good, and the oldest is some 900 years later than Caesar's day.

Of the 142 books of the *Roman History* of Livy (59 B.C.E.-17 C.E.) only thirty-five survived. These are known to us from not more than twenty manuscripts, only one of which is as old as the fourth century.

Of the fourteen books of the *Histories of Tacitus* (c. 100 C.E.) only four and a half survived. Of the sixteen books of his Annals, ten survived in full and two in part. The text of these existing portions of his two great historical works depends entirely on two manuscripts, one from the 9th century and one from the 11th Century.

*The History of Thucydides* (c. 480-400 B.C.E.) is known to us from eight manuscripts, the earliest written in 900 C.E.

Yet no classics scholar would listen to an argument that the authenticity of Herodotus or Thucydides is in doubt because the earliest manuscripts of their works, which are of any use to us, are over 1,300 years later than the originals.

The text of the New Testament is attested by manuscript testimony more voluminous in quantity and more reliable than that of any of the writings of the same period. Indeed there are no ancient writings whose evidence of a correct text is stronger than the New Testament. Personally, I feel that those scholars who hold that the Bible, both the Old and the New Testament, is not an historical document are displaying their blind prejudice.

# *What is a Jew?*

By S. OSTROVSKY

On the surface, this would seem an entirely superfluous question. Who does not know what and who is a Jew? And yet, is it not a fact that this very question has, in its religious and national aspects, claimed the attention of the Israeli public, and has even caused repeated crises in the State of Israel and its Government?

It is unlikely that this fundamental question will find a universally agreed and accepted answer before there is a spiritual revolution in Israel, and a completely new and fundamentally different approach to the Holy Scriptures, both the TENACH* and the New Testament.

I wish to cite a brief passage from the letter to the *Romans* by Saul-Paul of Tarsus, chapter 9, in the hope that it, along with the following exposition, will commend itself as a well-founded and true answer to the above question.

> I AM SPEAKING THE TRUTH IN MESSIAH (CHRIST), I AM NOT LYING; MY CONSCIENCE BEARS ME WITNESS IN THE HOLY SPIRIT, THAT I HAVE GREAT SORROW AND UNCEASING ANGUISH IN MY HEART. FOR I COULD WISH THAT I MYSELF WERE ACCURSED AND CUT OFF FROM CHRIST FOR THE SAKE OF MY BRETHREN, MY KINSMEN BY RACE. THEY ARE ISRAELITES, AND TO THEM

BELONG THE SONSHIP, THE GLORY, THE COVENANTS, THE GIVING OF THE LAW, THE WORSHIP, AND THE PROMISES; TO THEM BELONG THE PATRIARCHS, AND OF THEIR RACE, ACCORDING TO THE FLESH, IS THE CHRIST. GOD WHO IS OVER ALL BE BLESSED FOREVER. AMEN.

BUT IT IS NOT AS THOUGH THE WORDS OF GOD HAD FAILED. FOR NOT ALL WHO ARE DESCENDED FROM ISRAEL BELONG TO ISRAEL, AND NOT ALL ARE CHILDREN OF ABRAHAM BECAUSE THEY ARE HIS DESCENDANTS; BUT "THROUGH ISAAC SHALL YOUR DESCENDANTS BE NAMED." THIS MEANS THAT IT IS NOT THE CHILDREN OF THE FLESH WHO ARE THE CHILDREN OF GOD, BUT THE CHILDREN OF THE PROMISE ARE RECKONED AS DESCENDANTS.

FOR THIS IS WHAT THE PROMISE SAID, "ABOUT THIS TIME I WILL RETURN AND SARAH SHALL HAVE A SON." AND NOT ONLY SO, BUT ALSO WHEN REBECCA HAD CONCEIVED CHILDREN BY ONE MAN, OUR FOREFATHER ISAAC, THOUGH THEY WERE NOT YET BORN AND HAD DONE NOTHING EITHER GOOD OR BAD, IN ORDER THAT GOD'S PURPOSE OF ELECTION MIGHT CONTINUE, NOT BECAUSE OF WORKS BUT BECAUSE OF HIS CALL, SHE WAS TOLD, "THE ELDER WILL SERVE THE YOUNGER." AS IT IS WRITTEN, "JACOB I LOVED, BUT ESAU I HATED" (verses 1-13).

Not everyone born of Jewish parents is *ipso facto* a Jew, not even if Abraham himself were his father. Ishmael, the oldest son of Abraham, is declared not to have been a Jew, for it is written, "in Isaac shall seed be called to thee" (*Genesis* 21:12). True Jews are not the children of the flesh, but the children of promise.

But wasn't Ishmael the son of Abraham? Yes, however Hagar, his mother, was not a Jewess, and according to rabbinic law it is the national identity of the mother that determines the nationality of her offspring. According to this, Gershom, the son of our great teacher Moses, was not a Jew because his mother Zipporah was not a Jewess; and the heads of two tribes of Israel, Manasseh and Ephraim, were not Jews on account of their non-Jewish mother, Asenath, the daughter of Poti-phera (*Genesis*

41:50-52). There is no suggestion in the TENACH* that either Zipporah or Asenath became Jewish proselytes.

Saul-Paul comments on the birth of the two sons born to Rebecca, the wife of Isaac. One, Jacob, is a Jew, and the other, Esau, his twin brother, is not (*Romans* 9:6-8).

What is the principle that determines the Jewishness of Jacob and the non-Jewishness of his twin brother? There is one factor which alone determines who is a Jew. A Jew is one who, in addition to his Jewish descent, is also of "God's election," or in the words of Scripture, a man in line of the "sons of promise."

Something must be said about the national election of Israel and the position of the Jew as an individual. There is no doubt that Israel as a nation is a chosen people, and in this respect different from all other nations of the world:

> ISRAEL IS MY SON, MY FIRST-BORN ... THEN YE SHALL BE MINE OWN TREASURE FROM AMONG ALL PEOPLES; FOR ALL THE EARTH IS MINE; AND YE SHALL BE UNTO ME A KINGDOM OF PRIESTS, AND A HOLY NATION (*Exodus* 4:22; 19:5-6).
>
> THE PEOPLE WHICH I FORMED FOR MYSELF, THAT THEY MIGHT TELL OF MY PRAISE (*Isaiah* 43:21).
>
> MY DWELLING-PLACE ALSO SHALL BE OVER THEM; AND I WILL BE THEIR GOD, AND THEY SHALL BE MY PEOPLE. AND THE NATIONS SHALL KNOW THAT I AM THE LORD THAT SANCTIFY ISRAEL, WHEN MY SANCTUARY SHALL BE IN THE MIDST OF THEM FOREVER (*Ezekiel* 37:27-28).

The Russian writer Berdyaev set himself to the task of demonstrating from the histories of various nations the operation of materialistic principles in the development of these nations. When he came to the history of Israel he found it impossible to apply these principles. It led him to a thoughtful reading of the Bible and to his becoming a believer in God and His Messiah.

Truly, Israel differs from all other nations, for Israel, as a nation, has been chosen of God to give substance to God's plan of salvation for the whole world. However, when the Jew, as an individual, thinks that because of his Jewish descent he is the "elect of God," he is on false ground and deceives himself.

God chose the nation of Israel for a specific and exalted purpose—that through this nation salvation should come to the world. In this framework, Israel and the world have received and will yet receive all the highest spiritual values. But this does not mean that every individual Jew is a member of this national body which God has chosen for this exalted purpose. On the contrary, in every era of Jewish history only a small minority constituted the essence of God-chosen Israel. These, and these only, were the true Jews, "sons of God's election," or "sons of promise."

The vast majority of Israel at all times formed the national framework in which this Israel-essence was to be found. Thus the Prophet Elijah speaks plaintively to God, saying:

> I HAVE BEEN VERY JEALOUS FOR THE LORD, THE GOD OF HOSTS; FOR THE CHILDREN OF ISRAEL HAVE FORSAKEN THY COVENANT, THROWN DOWN THINE ALTARS, AND SLAIN THY PROPHETS WITH THE SWORD; AND I, EVEN I ONLY, AM LEFT; AND THEY SEEK MY LIFE, TO TAKE IT AWAY (*I Kings* 19:10).

True, there were 7,000 men who had not bowed to Baal in Elijah's day, but their total number constituted only a fraction of one percent of the nation as a whole. No doubt they were considered rather "peculiar" folk by their fellow-Jews of that day.

Isaiah similarly speaks of his day and says:

> FOR THOUGH THY PEOPLE, O ISRAEL, BE AS THE SAND OF THE SEA, ONLY A REMNANT OF THEM SHALL RETURN (*Isaiah* 10:22).

This can be said of most periods of Jewish history, that it was always a small remnant that constituted the essential nucleus of God's chosen people within the national framework of Israel.

In God's sight, this remnant, these were the people of His choice who could worthily bear the name, "Israel."

There is a controversy between Israel and God which has lasted now 2,000 years. Many of our people either deliberately ignore God and the special purpose for which God has chosen them, or are entirely oblivious of the same. They have completely severed their contact with all that gives Israel a specific and special place in the history of mankind. We are, of course, free to choose whatever we like for our lives, but Israel never was and never will be "like all the nations."

On the other hand, the Religious Sector of the people in the State of Israel assume the position of "The Chosen Race" and consider themselves successors to "The Seat of Moses and the prophets." To their credit let it be said that they played a big part in keeping Israel from being assimilated amongst the nations during the long centuries of the Diaspora, but in their rigid pharisaism they played no less a part in causing the Dispersion. They created the spiritual ghetto in the land of our fathers centuries before the creation of the ghetto.

There are ominous signs that these same leaders now wish to turn the land of Israel into a ghetto-state. Israel was destined to be a channel of blessing to the world. If we deny or refuse this Divine appointment, there is nothing but spiritual death for us. In *Ezekiel's* vision Israel is seen as a vast cemetery, covered with bones. "Very many . . . very dry" (37:1-2; 11).

Unlike other peoples, a Jew is not a person who belongs only to a certain national group. In addition to Jewish descent, a Jew has to be a "son of promise," or, like Jacob, a "son of God's election."

Throughout the TENACH* there is a cord of promise of the Messiah who would "Raise up the tribes of Jacob, and restore the offspring of Israel; I will also give thee for a light of the nations, that My salvation may be unto the end of the earth" (*Isaiah* 49:6).

You cannot speak of the salvation of Israel without the salvation of the world. Our patriarchs and prophets saw this in their own time. In *Genesis* 22:18 God said to Abraham, "And in thy seed shall all the nations of the earth be blessed." David raises his voice and says, "O praise the Lord, all ye nations; laud Him, all ye peoples. For His mercy is great toward us; and the truth of the Lord endureth forever. Hallelujah" (*Psalm* 117:1-2).

Messiah is the source of this blessing, and Israel was destined to be the pipeline through which this blessing should flow to the nations. A person of Jewish nationality has no right to call himself an Israelite unless he has this Messianic consciousness, unless through personal response to God he has come into the stream of this Messianic redemptive destiny whose source is Messiah himself.

But Israel never understood its Messiah, because Israel never understood its place in God's plans and purposes, its mission to the nations. Israel never understood its own Law which was given in order to reveal the holiness of God and the sinfulness of man. Israel never understood the nature of sin which reigns and rules in the hearts of man. Israel never understood the need for repentance and the nature of redemption which he needed.

Who, then is a Jew? To this question, as in the case of Jacob and Esau, it is God Himself that gives the answer. This is the undeniable right of the Creator of the world, this is the choice of a Sovereign God.

A Jew has to choose to be a Jew; he cannot be one only through the sheer incidence of birth. A Jew is not merely a unit of a certain national grouping, but one who has personally and out of conviction come into living touch with God. Only then is he a true Jew, a praiser of God.

The Jew who believes in the Messiah Jesus is a complete and true Jew. He has personally, in response to God's call, joined himself to the stream of Messianic redemptive destiny.

Such contact with God does not come by means of the Law, and certainly not through the instrumentality of Tradition—the commandments which have accumulated through the centuries. The Messiah Jesus is the way to God. "No one comes to the Father, but by me" (*John* 14:6). Jesus has solved the problem of sin which has always been the wall separating us from God.

You cannot very well tear out from the TENACH* *Isaiah* 53, or *Zechariah* 12:10, or *Psalm* 22, or *Daniel* 9. As long as the TENACH* is to be found in the State of Israel, and as long as

God's love is operative towards Israel, as long as the Spirit of God is brooding over the Land, there will be found Jews in whose hearts the love of truth will overcome their fear of man.

> BEHOLD, A DAY OF THE LORD COMETH ... AND HIS FEET SHALL STAND IN THAT DAY UPON THE MOUNT OF OLIVES, WHICH IS BEFORE JERUSALEM ON THE EAST, AND THE MOUNT OF OLIVES SHALL BE CLEFT IN THE MIDST THEREOF ... AND THERE SHALL BE ONE DAY WHICH SHALL BE KNOWN AS THE LORD'S, NOT DAY, AND NOT NIGHT; BUT IT SHALL COME TO PASS, THAT AT EVENING TIME THERE SHALL BE LIGHT ... AND THE LORD SHALL BE KING OVER ALL THE EARTH; IN THAT DAY SHALL THE LORD BE ONE, AND HIS NAME ONE (*Zechariah* 14).

Israel will then be the people of God, and God will say of them, "I will place salvation in Zion for Israel My glory" (*Isaiah* 46:13).

And all Israel shall weep and mourn and make confession to God in the words of the Prophet Zechariah.

> AND I WILL POUR OUT ON THE HOUSE OF DAVID AND ON THE INHABITANTS OF JERUSALEM, THE SPIRIT OF GRACE AND OF SUPPLICATION, SO THAT THEY WILL LOOK ON ME WHOM THEY HAVE PIERCED; AND THEY WILL MOURN FOR HIM, AS ONE MOURNS FOR AN ONLY SON, AND THEY WILL WEEP BITTERLY OVER HIM, LIKE THE BITTER WEEPING OVER A FIRST-BORN (12:10, NASB)

# "How Long?"

By MAX ISAAC REICH

We ought to be thankful that we have in the TENACH* not only hallelujah shouts, but also a witness to divine faithfulness, veracity, truth, and unfailing goodness. We have also groans, sighs, breakdowns in faith recorded, when sun, moon, and stars are hidden from sight; when the powers of heaven were shaken, and there were left apparently only the forsaken heavings and tossings of doubt and despair.

Take for instance the book of *Jeremiah,* the most autobiographical book in the TENACH.* It is largely a diary of a man's conversations with his God. Here was a man with the sensitive temperament of an artist, a poet, a student, who was made the storm center in one of the most perplexing periods of history when everything seemed out of gear, when every institution went down into wrack and ruin. For some forty years Jeremiah stood his ground for the holiness and truth of God and for the certainty of coming judgment upon Temple, throne, and nation, and against the "Peace! Peace!" preaching of false prophets, the corrupt and covetous priests, the princes who regarded him as a dangerous pacifist, and the unthinking crowd swayed by the clever slogans of self-seeking demagogues. To them he was an "iron pillar and a brazen wall" (1:18). But not so when he was alone with God. Read the outpourings of his heart, "Wherefore doth the way of the wicked prosper? Wherefore are all they secure that deal very treacherously?" (12:1). And, "Why is my pain perpetual, and my wound incurable, so that it refuseth to be healed? Wilt Thou indeed be unto me as a deceitful brook, as waters that fail?" (15:18).

What language to use with God!

Or take the book of *Job,* and listen to a man stripped of wealth, family, health, and worse of all, reputation, cursing the day of his birth, and crying out of confusion and anguish against what seemed to him injustice in God's government, hidden behind the cloud.

But these people stood up to their doubts and perplexities until they emerged into the sunshine again. Their world was much like ours. In externals it may have differed, but in fundamentals it has not changed. The human heart still cries out for love, the mind for truth, the spirit like a dove for a home and a resting place. We still protest against might crushing right; against the stultifying of personality from being an end in itself to being a means to an end, in the interest of tyrants, whether of individual autocrats or of a state stepping beyond its God-appointed bounds. We still feel that life is neither a comedy nor a tragedy; that infinite wisdom, one with infinite goodness, is life's potter; that not stern unbending law, nor blind fate, nor uncertain caprice, but sovereign love bends over the wheel of life in its revolutions, shaping and molding us, making and remaking, until at last, blessed be His name, we come forth as vessels to His praise answering to the design of His mastermind.

In the book of *Psalms* we enter into a different atmosphere than that which pervades the other books of the TENACH.* In the latter we listen to the speech of God to His people, whether it be directly as from Mount Sinai, or by the prophets, or by great acts of history.

In the *Psalms* we hear Israel speaking to God, echoing back what He had first spoken. It is this remarkable feature which has made the *Psalms* one of the most influential books of the TENACH.*

The Israel we listen to in the *Psalms* is the true, the inner Israel, the godly remnant, often a very small and despised remnant, in the midst of a people bent on backsliding, a people which never understood its calling and election, its mission and place in the divine plan.

The spiritual witness of Israel is the fruit of a fragment of the people. This suffering remnant kept the lamp of faith burning in the midst of pagan darkness from century to century. This remnant rallied to the anointed prophets and their ministry when it would seem as if they were ploughing a lonely furrow. It was for the sake of this living kernel that the shell was miraculously preserved.

And in the fullness of time this remnant became the matrix by which God's plan for mankind was realized: "I will also give thee for a light of the nations, that My salvation may be unto the end of the earth" (*Isaiah* 49:6).

Many of the *Psalms* are the outcome of perplexity. The heart of the seeker after God, baffled with the mysteries of life and death, often gave way before the unexplained and the inscrutable. Hence the repeated "Why?" "Wherefore?" and "How Long?" cry of the Psalmist. The latter has been called faith's mighty question, as it is really a confession that wrong cannot be permanent in a universe presided over by one whose throne is based on Justice and Right.

There are serious problems dealt with in the book of *Psalms.* There is the problem of pain, the mystery of suffering, particularly of the righteous! There is the shadow of death, an enemy as yet undefeated! There is the strange overthrow of the cause of God, as it seemed to the natural mind, when the heathen entered the House where His honor dwelt and destroyed it!

There is the cry out of the depths of self-discovery in the light of the divine holiness; the cry of repentance and penitence; the problem of moral evil! There is the hiding of the Face of God from one who has found in Him his supreme treasure; His strange silence to His worshipper, who feels lonely and bereaved without God as Friend and Guide; who is conscious that the world is a dry and thirsty land where there is no water; so that God alone is the source of his happiness, and the veiling of His radiant countenance an intolerable exile from the home of the soul!

The God of Israel hates sin and teaches those who seek Him to hate sin also. They find their secret sins exposed and rebuked (*Psalm* 90:8), "Thou hast set our iniquities before Thee, our secret sins in the light of Thy countenance." Hence the note of penitence in the book of *Psalms*. We meet with this phenomenon: the greater the person, the deeper his sense of sin. And then, flowing from this, the evangelical experience in the love that pardons, purifies the heart, restores the joy of salvation, puts a new song in the mouth of the one whose feet have been lifted out of the deep mire and placed upon a rock (*Psalms* 40-41).

This rapturous discovery of the Grace of God makes the one who has found it evangelistic. So *Psalm* 32 fulfills the vow of *Psalm* 51, "Then will I teach transgressors Thy ways; and sinners shall return unto Thee" (*Psalm* 51:15).

The psalmist could not get the full answer to his anxious inquiries in his day. That awaited the coming of Him who is the Light of the world. His cross is the key to all mystery. Strange that it should be so, for to the natural mind it is utter darkness and the greatest mystery of all, even defeat and disaster, the triumph of hate, the victory of evil over good. But to faith, it is full of light, the highest peak of love, patience, meekness, unselfishness, renunciation. It is the defeat of the powers of darkness. It is the laying of the sure foundation on which the hopes of humanity can rest and the universal reign of God be established.

The *Psalms* are shot through and through with the Messianic Hope. The first two psalms are one psalm in the ancient Hebrew manuscripts and in the Septuagint,* and are an introduction to the entire collection. If in the first part we meet with the Blessed Man who measures up to the holiness of the Law—and the only One who did so—the second part brings in the counsels of God to set Him as King over the nations, His sceptre extending to the uttermost parts of the earth. He is addressed in these words, "Thou art My son, this day have I begotten thee" (*Psalm* 2:7).

These things awaited "the fullness of time" when God sent forth His Son. This has changed everything for us. Light was given to the perplexed people in the TENACH,* if not all the light, yet sufficient light to travel by to the city which God is building for His own. But the things that happened to them are recorded for our learning. God had us in view in recording their spiritual heights and depths, their discipline and education, their sorrows and their joys, their defeats and their triumphs, their doubts and their jubilant certainties, that we, through the comfort and promises of the TENACH,* might have Hope.

# *Thirteen Articles of Faith*

*(The author of this Creed was J. I. Landsman, a distinguished Messianic Jew. The division of the Creed into thirteen sections follows the traditional Jewish Creed, better known as the Creed of Maimonides.)*

## Introduction

The teaching of the New Testament is not a newfangled religion. It is the religion of Moses, the prophets, and their followers, but with this difference: while the prophets longed and waited for the redemption which the Messiah would bring to Israel and the world, Messianic Jews, together with all true Christians, believe that the Messiah has come, and that Yeshua-Jesus is the true Messiah of Israel, and that he has brought the salvation which the prophets from Moses to Malachi prophesied.

The religion of the New Testament, therefore, is the old and pure religion of our nation with the confirmation of God's faithfulness in having kept the promises He made through the prophets.

1. I believe with perfect faith in the Lord God of Israel, the God of love and salvation, the creator of the heavens and the earth, and of all things seen and unseen. He is the One God and Father. Of Him, and through Him, and to Him are all things, and He is over all and with all and in all, and to Him belongs the glory forever. Amen.

2. I believe with perfect faith that God, blessed be His name, is a Spirit, and that true worshippers must worship their Father in heaven in spirit and in truth, for with such worshippers the Father is well pleased.

3. I believe with perfect faith in the Messiah Jesus our Lord, the only son, well-beloved of his Father in heaven, whom God raised up to be the Redeemer of Israel, as He promised our fathers by His holy prophets, who for us, the children of Adam, and for our salvation descended from heaven and became man.

He was conceived of the Holy Spirit, born of the Virgin Mary, of the seed of David, and was anointed of God with the Holy Spirit and with power. He was tempted in all things as we are, but without sin. He glorified his Father in heaven, and made known His name and His will to men. He walked about on earth doing good to the children of Israel.

He bore the reproach of sinners, and was afflicted even unto death, the death on the cross, the Righteous One for the wicked

He was wounded for our transgressions; he was bruised for our iniquities; the chastisement of our peace was upon him; and with his stripes we are healed.

Therefore has God highly exalted him, and raised him up again from the dead on the third day, after his death and burial. He showed himself openly to his disciples, and ascended into heaven, where he now sits at the right hand of God. From there he shall return a second time in glory to set up his kingdom, restore all things, and to judge the living and the dead.

He shall reign over the house of Jacob forever, and of his kingdom there shall be no end. Amen.

4. I believe with perfect faith that the Messiah Jesus, our Lord, is the image of the hidden God. He is the bright reflection of God's glory and the image of His being. He is before everything. He is the power of God and the wisdom of God. In him dwells the fullness of the Godhead bodily, and in him are hid all the treasures of wisdom and knowledge. He that sees him sees the Father who is in heaven. He is the way and the truth and the life. No man can come to the Father except through him.

5. I believe with perfect faith that for us first God raised up the Messiah Jesus, and sent him to bless and to save his people from all their sins; and although our fathers rebelled and transgressed, yet God did not forsake His people, but exalted Jesus to be a Prince and a Saviour, to proclaim repentance to Israel, and the forgiveness of sins to everyone who believes on the name of Jesus the Messiah with a true and perfect heart.

6. I believe with perfect faith that by God's foreordained counsel and everlasting foreknowledge, our fathers rebelled against the Messiah Jesus, the King of Israel and His glory, in order that through their transgression salvation might come to the Gentiles, that they might be brought near to God and to His salvation in the Messiah. But when the fullness of the Gentiles shall be gathered into the Kingdom of heaven, then all Israel shall be saved with an everlasting salvation, and the Lord shall be King over all the earth.

7. I believe with perfect faith that the Messiah by his death, when he offered himself as an atonement for the sins of the whole world, fulfilled the law of commandments and ordinances, the source of enmity between Jews and Gentiles, and

destroyed the middle wall of partition, reconciling both unto God. And he created of the two one new man, and made peace between them. And now there is neither Jew nor Greek, neither slave nor free, neither male nor female, but all are one in the Messiah Jesus.

8. I believe with perfect faith that the Messiah is the end of the Torah* for righteousness to all who believe in him, and that by faith in the Messiah a person shall be justified before God without the works of the Torah;* for by the works of the Torah* no person of flesh and blood can be justified or made complete.

9. I believe with perfect faith that in the Messiah Jesus neither circumcision nor uncircumcision counts for anything, but a new creation and faith which works from love. For love out of a pure heart is the end of the whole Torah* and its true fulfillment, and whoever is in the Messiah is a new creation created to good deeds.

10. I believe with perfect faith in the Holy Spirit, the Comforter, who dwells forever with them that believe, to sanctify them and to lead them into all truth.

11. I believe with perfect faith that God spoke to our fathers through the prophets; and in the last days He spoke to us by His Son, Jesus the Messiah, and that both alike are words of the living God.

12. I believe with perfect faith that the Holy Scriptures which we now possess were written under the inspiration of the Holy Spirit, and are able to make us wise unto salvation through faith in the Messiah Jesus, and to lead us in the way of righteousness so that we may be perfect and be prepared for every good work.

13. I believe with perfect faith in one holy congregation, a congregation of true believers, built on the foundation of the apostles and prophets, and on the Messiah Jesus who is the Cornerstone.

I confess one baptism for the forgiveness of sins. I wait for the resurrection from the dead, and for life everlasting. Amen.

* * *

(We have seen the true Light; we have received the Spirit from on high. The true faith is our precious possession through our Redeemer. Blessed be our faithful God from everlasting to everlasting. Amen.)

# עקרי אמונתנו הקדושה

א. אני מאמין באמונה שלמה ביהוה אלהי ישראל · אלהי האהבה והישועה · בורא שמים וארץ ואת־כל־הנראים ואשר אינם נראים : הוא אל ואב אחד · ממנו ועל ידו ואליו הכל · והוא על־כל ואת־כל ובתוך כל · ולו הכבוד לעולמים · אמן :

ב. אני מאמין באמונה שלמה שהאלהים יתברך שמו רוח הוא ושעבדי אל האמתים צריכים להשתחות לאביהם שבשמים ברוח ובאמת כי במשתחוים כאלה חפץ האב :

ג. אני מאמין באמונה שלמה במשיח ישוע אדונינו · הבן היחיד והאהוב לאביו שבשמים · אשר הקים אתו האלהים גואל לישראל · כפי ההבטחה לאבותינו על ידי נביאיו הקדושים : אשר למעננו בני אדם ולמען ישועתנו ירד מן השמים ויהי לבן־האדם · נוצר מרוח הקדש · נולד ממרים העלמה · מזרע בית דוד · נמשח מאת האלהים ברוח הקדש ובגבורה · נתנסה בכל כמנו ובלי־חטא · פאר את־אביו שבשמים · הודיע את־שמו ואת־רצונו לבני האדם · התהלך בארץ עשה חסד עם־כל בני ישראל · נשא כלמה גדולה מאת החטאים ויענה עד מות · עד מיתת הצליבה · הצדיק בעד הרשעים : על כן הגביהו האלהים מאד וביום השלישי אחרי מותו וקבורתו הקים אתו מן המתים ויתנהו להראות בגלוי לתלמידיו ויושיבהו ליד ימינו במרומים · ומשם יבא שנית בכבוד · להכין את־ממלכתו · להשיב כל־הדברים לתקונם · ולשפט את־החיים ואת המתים · והוא מלך על בית יעקב לעולם ולמלכותו אין קץ · אמן :

ד. אני מאמין באמונה שלמה שהמשיח ישוע אדונינו הוא צלם האלהים הנעלם · זהר כבודו וצלם עצמותו · קדמון לכל־דבר · גבורת אלהים וחכמתו : בו שוכן כל מלוא האלהות ונגוזים כל אצרות החכמה והדעת : הראה אתו יחזה את־אבינו שבשמים : הוא הדרך והאמת והחיים · לא יבא איש אל־האב בלתי על ידו :

ה. אני מאמין באמונה שלמה כי לנו בראשונה העמיד האלהים את־ישוע המשיח וישלחהו לברך ולהושיע את־עמו מכל חטאתיו : ואף־כי אבותינו מרדו ופשעו בו · לא זנח האלהים את־עמו · כי־אם נשא את ישוע לשר ולמושיע · לתת תשובה לישראל וסליחת החטאים · לכל המאמין בשם ישוע המשיח באמת ובלב תמים :

ז. אני מאמין באמונה שלמה שעל פי עצת האלהים הנחרצה וידיעתו מקדם מרדו אבותינו במשיח ישוע · מלך ישראל ותפארתו · למען בפשעם תבא הישועה לגוים · לקרב אותם לאלהים ולישועתו במשיח · למען תמלא הארץ דעה את־יהוה : אכן כאשר יכנס מלוא הגוים לתוך מלכות השמים · אז כל־ישראל יושע תשועת עולמים · והיה יהוה למלך על כל־הארץ :

ז. אני מאמין באמונה שלמה שהמשיח על־ידי צליבתו · בהקריבו את־נפשו לכפרה על חטאת כל־העולם · בטל את־תורת המצות והחקות · מקור האיבה בין היהודים והגוים · והרס מחיצת הגדר · וירצה את־שניהם לאלהים · ויברא את־השנים לאדם אחד חדש · ויעש שלום ביניהם : ואין עוד יהודי ולא יוני · אין עבד ולא בן־חורין · אין זכר ולא נקבה · כי כלם אחד המה במשיח ישוע :

ח. אני מאמין באמונה שלמה שהמשיח סוף התורה הוא לצדקה לכל־המאמין בו · ושבאמונת המשיח יצדק האדם לפני האלהים · בבלי מעשי תורה · כי ממעשי התורה לא יצדק ולא יושלם כל־בשר :

ט. אני מאמין באמונה שלמה שבמשיח ישוע לא המילה תחשב ולא הערלה כי־אם הבריאה החדשה והאמונה הפעלת באהבה · כי האהבה בלב טהור היא תכלית התורה כלה וקיומה האמתי : ומי שהוא במשיח בריה חדשה הוא · נברא לחיי קדושה ולמעשים טובים :

י. אני מאמין באמונה שלמה ברוח הקדש הפרקלית · אשר ישכן את־המאמינים לנצח · יקדש וידריך אותם אל האמת כלה :

יא. אני מאמין באמונה שלמה שהאלהים דבר אל אבותינו ביד הנביאים · ובאחרית הימים דבר אלינו בבנו ישוע המשיח · ואלו ואלו דברי אלהים חיים :

יב· אני מאמין באמונה שלמה שכתבי הקדש הנמצאים עתה בידינו נכתבו ברוח הקדש · ונכנים להחכימנו לישועת על־ידי האמונה במשיח ישוע ולהדריכנו במעגלי צדק · למען נהיה תמימים ומוכנים לכל־מעשה טוב :

יג. אני מאמין באמונה שלמה בכנסיה אחת קדושה וכללית עדת הקדושים · הבנויה על־יסוד השליחים והנביאים וישוע המשיח הוא אבן פנתה :

מודה אני בטבילה אחת לסליחת החטאים : מחכה אני לתחית המתים ולחיי עולם הבא · אמן :

ראינו אור אמת · לקחנו רוח משיח · קנינו אמונת־אמת · על־ידי גואלנו אמת : ברוך אלהי־אמת שמו וחסדו לעולמי עולמים · אמן :

ו אֲנִי מַאֲמִין בֶּאֱמוּנָה שְׁלֵמָה שֶׁעַל פִּי עֲצַת הָאֱלֹהִים הַנֶּחֱרָצָה וִידִיעָתוֹ מִקֶּדֶם מָרְדוּ אֲבוֹתֵינוּ בַּמָּשִׁיחַ יֵשׁוּעַ · מֶלֶךְ יִשְׂרָאֵל וְתִפְאַרְתּוֹ · לְמַעַן בְּפִשְׁעָם תָּבֹא הַיְשׁוּעָה לַגּוֹיִם · לְקָרֵב אוֹתָם לֵאלֹהִים וְלִישׁוּעָתוֹ בַּמָּשִׁיחַ · לְמַעַן תִּמָּלֵא הָאָרֶץ דֵּעָה אֶת־יְהוָֹה : אָכֵן כַּאֲשֶׁר יִכָּנֵס מְלוֹא הַגּוֹיִם לְתוֹךְ מַלְכוּת הַשָּׁמַיִם · אָז כָּל־יִשְׂרָאֵל יִוָּשַׁע תְּשׁוּעַת עוֹלָמִים · וְהָיָה יְהוָֹה לְמֶלֶךְ עַל כָּל־הָאָרֶץ :

ז אֲנִי מַאֲמִין בֶּאֱמוּנָה שְׁלֵמָה שֶׁהַמָּשִׁיחַ עַל יְדֵי צְלִיבָתוֹ · בְּהַקְרִיבוֹ אֶת־נַפְשׁוֹ לְכַפָּרָה עַל חַטֹּאת כָּל־הָעוֹלָם · בִּטֵּל אֶת־תּוֹרַת הַמִּצְוֹת וְהַחֻקּוֹת · מְקוֹר הָאֵיבָה בֵּין הַיְּהוּדִים וְהַגּוֹיִם · וְהָרַס מְחִיצַת הַגָּדֵר · וַיְרַצֶּה אֶת־שְׁנֵיהֶם לֵאלֹהִים · וַיִּבְרָא אֶת־הַשְּׁנַיִם לְאָדָם אֶחָד חָדָשׁ · וַיַּעַשׂ שָׁלוֹם בֵּינֵיהֶם : וְאֵין עוֹד יְהוּדִי וְלֹא יְוָנִי · אֵין עֶבֶד וְלֹא בֶּן־חוֹרִין · אֵין זָכָר וְלֹא נְקֵבָה · כִּי כוּלָּם אֶחָד הֵמָּה בַּמָּשִׁיחַ יֵשׁוּעַ :

ח אֲנִי מַאֲמִין בֶּאֱמוּנָה שְׁלֵמָה שֶׁהַמָּשִׁיחַ סוֹף הַתּוֹרָה הוּא לִצְדָקָה לְכָל־הַמַּאֲמִין בּוֹ · וְשֶׁבֶּאֱמוּנַת הַמָּשִׁיחַ יִצְדַּק הָאָדָם לִפְנֵי הָאֱלֹהִים · בִּבְלִי מַעֲשֵׂי תוֹרָה · כִּי מִמַּעֲשֵׂי הַתּוֹרָה לֹא יִצְדַּק וְלֹא יוּשְׁלַם כָּל־בָּשָׂר :

ט אֲנִי מַאֲמִין בֶּאֱמוּנָה שְׁלֵמָה שֶׁבַּמָּשִׁיחַ יֵשׁוּעַ לֹא הַמִּילָה תֵחָשֵׁב וְלֹא הָעָרְלָה כִּי־אִם הַבְּרִיאָה הַחֲדָשָׁה וְהָאֱמוּנָה הַפֹּעֶלֶת בְּאַהֲבָה · כִּי הָאַהֲבָה בְּלֵב טָהוֹר הִיא תַּכְלִית הַתּוֹרָה כּוּלָּהּ וְקִיּוּמָהּ הָאֲמִתִּי : וּמִי שֶׁהוּא בַּמָּשִׁיחַ בְּרִיָּה חֲדָשָׁה הוּא · נִבְרָא לְמַעֲשִׂים טוֹבִים :

י אֲנִי מַאֲמִין בֶּאֱמוּנָה שְׁלֵמָה בְּרוּחַ הַקֹּדֶשׁ הַפְּרַקְלִיט · אֲשֶׁר יִשְׁכֹּן אֶת־הַמַּאֲמִינִים לָנֶצַח · יְקַדֵּשׁ וְיַדְרִיךְ אוֹתָם אֶל הָאֱמֶת כּוּלָּהּ :

יא אֲנִי מַאֲמִין בֶּאֱמוּנָה שְׁלֵמָה שֶׁהָאֱלֹהִים דִּבֶּר אֶל אֲבוֹתֵינוּ בְּיַד הַנְּבִיאִים · וּבְאַחֲרִית הַיָּמִים דִּבֶּר אֵלֵינוּ בִּבְנוֹ יֵשׁוּעַ הַמָּשִׁיחַ · וְאֵלּוּ וָאֵלּוּ דִּבְרֵי אֱלֹהִים חַיִּים :

יב אֲנִי מַאֲמִין בֶּאֱמוּנָה שְׁלֵמָה שֶׁכִּתְבֵי הַקֹּדֶשׁ הַנִּמְצָאִים עַתָּה בְּיָדֵינוּ נִכְתְּבוּ בְּרוּחַ הַקֹּדֶשׁ · וּנְכֹנִים לְהַחֲכִימֵנוּ לִישׁוּעָה עַל־יְדֵי הָאֱמוּנָה בַּמָּשִׁיחַ יֵשׁוּעַ וּלְהַדְרִיכֵנוּ בְּמַעְגְּלֵי צֶדֶק · לְמַעַן נִהְיֶה תְמִימִים וּמוּכָנִים לְכָל־מַעֲשֶׂה טוֹב :

יג אֲנִי מַאֲמִין בֶּאֱמוּנָה שְׁלֵמָה בִּכְנֵסִיָּה אַחַת קְדוֹשָׁה וּכְלָלִית עֲדַת הַקְּדוֹשִׁים · הַבְּנוּיָה עַל־יְסוֹד הַשְּׁלִיחִים וְהַנְּבִיאִים וְיֵשׁוּעַ הַמָּשִׁיחַ הוּא אֶבֶן פִּנָּתָהּ :

מוֹדֶה אֲנִי בִּטְבִילָה אַחַת לִסְלִיחַת הַחֲטָאִים : מְחַכֶּה אֲנִי לִתְחִיַּת הַמֵּתִים וּלְחַיֵּי עוֹלָם הַבָּא : אָמֵן :

תם

# עִקְּרֵי אֱמוּנָתֵנוּ הַקְּדוֹשָׁה

א אֲנִי מַאֲמִין בֶּאֱמוּנָה שְׁלֵמָה בַּיהוָה אֱלֹהֵי יִשְׂרָאֵל · אֱלֹהֵי הָאַהֲבָה וְהַיְשׁוּעָה · בּוֹרֵא שָׁמַיִם וָאָרֶץ וְאֶת־כָּל הַנִּרְאִים וַאֲשֶׁר אֵינָם נִרְאִים : הוּא אֵל וְאָב אֶחָד · מִמֶּנּוּ וְעַל יָדוֹ וְאֵלָיו הַכֹּל · וְהוּא עַל־כֹּל וְאֶת־כֹּל וּבְתוֹךְ כֹּל · וְלוֹ הַכָּבוֹד לְעוֹלָמִים · אָמֵן :

ב אֲנִי מַאֲמִין בֶּאֱמוּנָה שְׁלֵמָה שֶׁהָאֱלֹהִים יִתְבָּרַךְ שְׁמוֹ רוּחַ הוּא וְשֶׁעֹבְדֵי אֵל הָאֲמִתִּים צְרִיכִים לְהִשְׁתַּחֲוֹת לַאֲבִיהֶם שֶׁבַּשָּׁמַיִם בְּרוּחַ וּבֶאֱמֶת כִּי בְּמִשְׁתַּחֲוִים כָּאֵלֶּה חָפֵץ הָאָב :

ג אֲנִי מַאֲמִין בֶּאֱמוּנָה שְׁלֵמָה בַּמָּשִׁיחַ יֵשׁוּעַ אֲדוֹנֵינוּ · הַבֵּן הַיָּחִיד וְהָאָהוּב לְאָבִיו שֶׁבַּשָּׁמַיִם · אֲשֶׁר הֵקִים אֹתוֹ הָאֱלֹהִים גּוֹאֵל לְיִשְׂרָאֵל · כְּפִי הַהַבְטָחָה לַאֲבוֹתֵינוּ עַל יְדֵי נְבִיאָיו הַקְּדוֹשִׁים : אֲשֶׁר לְמַעֲנֵנוּ בְּנֵי אָדָם וּלְמַעַן יְשׁוּעָתֵנוּ יָרַד מִן הַשָּׁמַיִם וַיְהִי לְבֶן־הָאָדָם · נוֹצַר מֵרוּחַ הַקֹּדֶשׁ · נוֹלַד מִמִּרְיָם הָעַלְמָה · מִזֶּרַע בֵּית דָּוִד · נִמְשַׁח מֵאֵת הָאֱלֹהִים בְּרוּחַ הַקֹּדֶשׁ וּבִגְבוּרָה · נִתְנַסָּה בַּכֹּל כָּמֹנוּ וּבְלִי־חֵטְא · פֵּאֵר אֶת־אָבִיו שֶׁבַּשָּׁמַיִם · הוֹדִיעַ אֶת־שְׁמוֹ וְאֶת־רְצוֹנוֹ לִבְנֵי הָאָדָם · הִתְהַלֵּךְ בָּאָרֶץ עֹשֶׂה חֶסֶד עִם־כָּל בְּנֵי יִשְׂרָאֵל · נָשָׂא כְלִמָּה גְדוֹלָה מֵאֵת הַחַטָּאִים וַיְעוּנֶּה עַד מָוֶת · עַד מִתַת הַצְּלִיבָה · הַצַּדִּיק בְּעַד הָרְשָׁעִים : וְהוּא מְחֹלָל מִפְּשָׁעֵינוּ מְדוּכָּא מֵעֲוֹנֹתֵינוּ מוּסַר שְׁלוֹמֵנוּ עָלָיו וּבַחֲבוּרָתוֹ נִרְפָּא לָנוּ : עַל כֵּן הִגְבִּיהוֹ הָאֱלֹהִים מְאֹד וּבַיּוֹם הַשְּׁלִישִׁי אַחֲרֵי מוֹתוֹ וּקְבוּרָתוֹ הֵקִים אֹתוֹ מִן הַמֵּתִים וַיִּתְּנֵהוּ לְהֵרָאוֹת בַּגָּלוּי לְתַלְמִידָיו וַיּוֹשִׁיבֵהוּ לְיַד יְמִינוֹ בַּמְּרוֹמִים · וּמִשָּׁם יָבֹא שֵׁנִית בְּכָבוֹד לְהָכִין אֶת־מַמְלַכְתּוֹ · לְהָשִׁיב כָּל־הַדְּבָרִים לְתִקּוּנָם · וְלִשְׁפֹּט אֶת־הַחַיִּים וְאֶת־הַמֵּתִים · וְהוּא מֶלֶךְ עַל בֵּית יַעֲקֹב לְעוֹלָם וּלְמַלְכוּתוֹ אֵין קֵץ · אָמֵן :

ד אֲנִי מַאֲמִין בֶּאֱמוּנָה שְׁלֵמָה שֶׁהַמָּשִׁיחַ יֵשׁוּעַ אֲדוֹנֵינוּ הוּא צֶלֶם הָאֱלֹהִים הַנֶּעְלָם · זֹהַר כְּבוֹדוֹ וְצֶלֶם עַצְמוּתוֹ · קַדְמוֹן לְכָל דָּבָר · גְּבוּרַת אֱלֹהִים וְחָכְמָתוֹ · בּוֹ שׁוֹכֵן כָּל מְלוֹא הָאֱלָהוּת וּגְנוּזִים כָּל אֹצְרוֹת הַחָכְמָה וְהַדָּעַת : הָרֹאֶה אֹתוֹ יֶחֱזֶה אֶת־אָבִינוּ שֶׁבַּשָּׁמָיִם : הוּא הַדֶּרֶךְ וְהָאֱמֶת וְהַחַיִּים · לֹא יָבֹא אִישׁ אֶל־הָאָב בִּלְתִּי עַל יָדוֹ :

ה אֲנִי מַאֲמִין בֶּאֱמוּנָה שְׁלֵמָה כִּי לָנוּ בָּרִאשׁוֹנָה הֶעֱמִיד הָאֱלֹהִים אֶת־יֵשׁוּעַ הַמָּשִׁיחַ וַיְשַׁלְּחֵהוּ לְבָרֵךְ וּלְהוֹשִׁיעַ אֶת־עַמּוֹ מִכָּל חַטֹּאתָיו · וְאַף־כִּי אֲבוֹתֵינוּ מָרְדוּ וּפָשְׁעוּ בוֹ · לֹא זָנַח הָאֱלֹהִים אֶת־עַמּוֹ · כִּי־אִם נִשָּׂא אֶת יֵשׁוּעַ לְשַׂר וּלְמוֹשִׁיעַ · לָתֵת תְּשׁוּבָה לְיִשְׂרָאֵל וּסְלִיחַת הַחֲטָאִים · לְכָל־הַמַּאֲמִין בְּשֵׁם יֵשׁוּעַ הַמָּשִׁיחַ בֶּאֱמֶת וּבְלֵב תָּמִים :

# *Jesus was not a Christian*

By JOHN MURRAY SMOOT

Jesus was not a Christian? Wasn't he the first Christian . . . who started a whole new religion? No, Jesus could not have been a Christian simply because people didn't start name-calling his followers that way until years after his death (*The Acts of the Apostles* 11:26).

And Jesus certainly wouldn't have been recognized as a Christian throughout his entire life. He was circumcised on the eighth day after his birth, was presented for purification in the Temple in Jerusalem, and was thoroughly indoctrinated in the sacred Jewish writings (*Luke* 2:21-24).

He could trace his Davidic lineage all the way back to Abraham (*Matthew* 1:1-16). Jesus, who lived during the time of the Second Temple, scrupulously adhered to the law of Moses, kept the high feasts, paid the Temple half-shekel, and enjoined his disciples to keep every detail of the TORAH.*

His disputations with the rationalism of the Sadducees and the midrashic overlayment of the Rabbis are legendary.

It may startle one to reflect that Jesus strictly forbade his followers from calling him the Messiah (*Matthew* 16:20; *Luke* 9:20, 21). Why would Jesus reject the use of that title? Simply because it had attracted to itself by that time a completely erroneous coloring. Rabbinic Judaism had painted a monochromatic portrait of Messiah that was wholly political. The Bar Kokhba Revolt, led by a messianic figure called Bar Kokhba, son of the Star, instigated an armed insurrection against the imperial rule of Hadrian. The attempt was bloodily suppressed in 135 C.E. and was later to personify this concept. Jesus utterly refused to be identified with this kind of politically-oriented figure. "My kingship is not of this world," he testified to Pontius Pilate. "If my kingship were of this world, my servants would fight, that I might not be handed over . . . " (*John* 18:36)

If Jesus rejected the misuse of the title of Messiah, what designation did he choose for himself? . . . the deliberately ambiguous *Son of Man.* He never attempted to define the term, but those who knew the Scriptures would sense the double meaning. In *Daniel* chapter 7, verse 13, he is seen as the glorious cloudrider coming and reigning over all peoples in the name of the Ancient of Days. The Son of Man was God's worthy prophet. Yet the term also applied to the humble and humiliated suffering servant of the Lord, witnessed to by the prophets. *Isaiah* 52:13 begins, "Behold, my servant . . ."

Jonathan ben Uzziel, a disciple of Hillel who lived early in the second century C. E., opens his Targum* with, "Behold, my servant Messiah . . ." This servant is seen as a man of sorrows, who was "wounded because of our transgressions, he was crushed because of our iniquities" (*Isaiah* 53:5). But after being the suffering, silent saviour, he is exalted as the bringer of spiritual prosperity.

God, our Father, would not suffer His godly one to see the pit (*Psalm* 16:10), but raised him at his own right hand (*Matthew* 26:64).

No, Jesus was not a Christian but Jews and Gentiles who have entrusted themselves to him have found the way to the one, true, living God.

# *A Case of*

# *Mistaken Identity*

By RACHMIEL FRYDLAND

Much has been written and discussed about the section of *Isaiah* 52:13 to 53:12 in the TENACH.* The passage speaks of an outstanding servant of the Lord whose visage is marred from suffering, and who is afflicted and stricken through the transgressions of my people, i.e. the Prophet Isaiah's. He has not deserved any pain or wounds, but was wounded because of our transgressions, crushed because of our iniquities, and with his stripes we were healed.

Not only is He concerned with us, the Jewish people, but He will also startle many nations who will be cleansed from their evil and sins through His sufferings. Even Gentile kings and rulers will give Him a hearing.

The chapters preceding and following the passage also speak of the physical and spiritual cleansing and salvation of Israel. Thus in *Isaiah* 52:10 we see God's concern, first with Israel, and then with the Gentiles:

> THE LORD HATH MADE BARE HIS HOLY ARM IN THE EYES OF ALL THE NATIONS; AND ALL THE ENDS OF THE EARTH SHALL SEE THE SALVATION OF OUR GOD.

God who created all nations is concerned for the salvation of all nations. Besides, there is no safety for Israel unless the nations also acknowledge the God of Israel. The same is true of the chapters that follow this passage wherein Israel is admonished to:

> ENLARGE THE PLACE OF THY TENT, AND LET THEM STRETCH FORTH THE CURTAINS OF THY HABITATIONS, SPARE NOT; LENGTHEN THY CORDS, AND STRENGTHEN THY STAKES. FOR THOU SHALT SPREAD ABROAD ON THE RIGHT HAND AND ON THE LEFT; AND THY SEED SHALL POSSESS THE NATIONS (*Isaiah* 54:2-3).

This theme is carried over to the next chapter where everyone is invited to drink and feast on the spiritual food of God:

> BEHOLD, I HAVE GIVEN HIM FOR A WITNESS TO THE PEOPLE, A PRINCE AND COMMANDER TO THE PEOPLES. BEHOLD, THOU SHALT CALL A NATION THAT THOU KNOWEST NOT, AND A NATION THAT KNEW NOT THEE SHALL RUN UNTO THEE (*Isaiah* 55:4-5).

Clearly this statement speaks of God's anointed One, the Messiah, who is interested in the salvation and justification of Israel, and then in the salvation of the other nations—the Gentiles.

The text and context present the suffering Servant of the Lord God who dies as a *Korban,* a sacrifice for guilt. He is then buried with the rich and wicked, but is gloriously resurrected to life. God permits His afflicted Servant to endure this suffering in order to effect the removal of the sins of many, the Jew first, and also the Gentile.

Among our ancient commentators there is a consensus of

opinion regarding these passages. The Aramaic translation ascribed to Rabbi Jonathan ben Uzziel, a disciple of Hillel who lived early in the second century C. E., begins with these words:

> BEHOLD, MY SERVANT MESSIAH SHALL PROSPER; HE SHALL BE HIGH, AND INCREASE, AND BE EXCEEDING STRONG: AS THE HOUSE OF ISRAEL LOOKED TO HIM THROUGH MANY DAYS, BECAUSE THEIR COUNTENANCE WAS DARKENED AMONG THE PEOPLES, AND THEIR COMPLEXION BEYOND THE SONS OF MEN.

We find the same interpretation in the Babylonian Talmud,* *Sanhedrin* 98*b:*

> WHAT IS HIS (THE MESSIAH'S) NAME? . . . THE RABBIS SAID: HIS NAME IS "THE LEPER SCHOLAR," AS IT IS WRITTEN, SURELY HE HATH BORNE OUR GRIEFS, AND CARRIED OUR SORROWS: YET WE DID ESTEEM HIM A LEPER, SMITTEN OF GOD, AND AFFLICTED.

Similarly in the *Midrash Rabbah* in an explanation of *Ruth* 2:14:

> HE IS SPEAKING OF THE KING MESSIAH: "COME HITHER" DRAW NEAR TO THE THRONE; "AND EAT OF THE BREAD," THAT IS, THE BREAD OF THE KINGDOM; "AND DIP THY MORSEL IN THE VINEGAR." THIS REFERS TO THE CHASTISEMENTS, AS IT IS SAID, "BUT HE WAS WOUNDED FOR OUR TRANSGRESSIONS, BRUISED FOR OUR INIQUITIES."

In the same manner also in the *Yalkut,* a later midrash:*

> WHO ART THOU, O GREAT MOUNTAIN? (*Zechariah* 4:7). THIS REFERS TO THE KING MESSIAH. AND WHY DOES HE CALL HIM THE "GREAT MOUNTAIN?" BECAUSE HE IS GREATER THAN THE PATRIARCHS, AS IT IS SAID, "MY SERVANT SHALL BE HIGH, AND LIFTED UP, AND LOFTY EXCEEDINGLY." HE WILL BE HIGHER THAN ABRAHAM WHO SAYS, "I HAVE LIFTED UP MY HAND UNTO THE LORD" (*Genesis* 14:22); LOFTIER THAN THE MINISTERING ANGELS, OF WHOM IT IS WRITTEN, "THEIR RINGS WERE HIGH AND DREADFUL" (*Ezekiel* 1:18). AND OUT OF WHOM DOES HE COME FORTH? "OUT OF DAVID" (*Yalkut* Vol. 2:571).

Although our ancient authorities interpreted this passage as referring to Messiah, some of the later Rabbis, of whom the most prominent was Rashi (short for Rabbi Shlomo Yitzhaki,

1040-1105), began to interpret the passage as referring to Israel. They knew that the older interpretations referred it to Messiah, but probably because of the pressures of a degenerate medieval Christianity, they wanted to preserve their people from accepting such a faith.

Their intentions were no doubt sincere; however, other prominent Jewish Rabbis and leaders realized the inconsistencies of Rashi's interpretation. They presented a threefold justified objection to his innovation. First, they pointed out the consensus of ancient opinion. Secondly, they pointed out that the text is in the singular. Thirdly, they pointed to *Isaiah* 53, verse 8, "For the transgression of my people to whom the stroke was due," and said that "my people" must be Israel for whom the Lord's servant suffers.

R. Mosheh Kohen Ibn Crispin explains the section:

"This passage, the commentators explain, speaks of the captivity of Israel, although the singular number is used in it throughout . . . Others have supposed it to mean the just in this present world who are crushed and oppressed now . . . but these too, for the same reason, by altering the number distort the verses from their natural meaning. And then it seemed to me that . . . having forsaken the knowledge of our Teachers, and inclined 'after the stubbornness of their own hearts,' and of their own opinion, I am pleased to interpret it, in accordance with the teaching of our Rabbis, of the King Messiah."

For the same reason, R. Mosheh El-Sheikh, Rabbi of Safed in the late sixteenth century, points out this truth, saying:

"I may remark, then, that our Rabbis with one voice accept and affirm the opinion that the prophet is speaking of the King Messiah."

Much to the point is the commentary of the great Jewish educator, Herz Homberg (1749-1841), who says:

"According to the opinion of Rashi and Ibn Ezra, it relates to Israel at the end of their captivity . . . but if so, what can be the meaning of the passage, 'He was wounded for our transgression?' Who was wounded? Who are the transgressors? Who carried the sickness and bore the pain? . . . The fact is that it refers to King Messiah."

The ones who interpreted the passage as referring to Israel had an insurmountable difficulty in *Isaiah* 53, verse 8, which reads:

> BY OPPRESSION AND JUDGMENT HE WAS TAKEN AWAY, AND WITH HIS GENERATION WHO DID REASON? FOR HE WAS CUT OFF OUT OF THE LAND OF THE LIVING, FOR THE TRANSGRESSION OF MY PEOPLE TO WHOM THE STROKE WAS DUE."

Were the Jewish people, God forbid, ever cut off from the land of the living? No! We are proud that *Am Yisrael Chai,* the people of Israel, live! In *Jeremiah* 31:35-37 God promised that they will exist forever.

It is impossible to say that Israel suffered for the transgressions of "my people" which clearly means Isaiah's people. Surely Isaiah's people are not the Gentiles, but the Jews. Consistency demands that we interpret this chapter as referring to Messiah.

Doubtless it is little known how *Oz M'lifnai B'reshis,* one of the prayers for *Yom Kippur,** came to be incorporated into the Jewish Prayer Book. Students of our liturgy are of the opinion that the prayer is a Judeo-Christian infiltration into the poesy of the Synagogal liturgy, else what explanation is there for this strange petition from *Musaf l'Yom Kippur:*

"Our righteous Messiah has departed from us. We are horror-stricken and have none to justify us. Upon his shoulders he carried our sins, and through his wounds we find forgiveness. O, Eternal One, create him anew. From Seir let come the Redeemer, from Mt. Lebanon let him proclaim redemption a second time through thy servant, Yinnon" (one of Messiah's names will be Yinnon according to rabbinic interpretation of *Psalm* 72:19).

„פָּנָה מֶנּוּ מְשִׁיחַ צִדְקֵנוּ. פְּלַצְנוּ וְאֵין מִי לְצַדְּקֵנוּ. עֲוֹנוֹתֵינוּ וְעוֹל־
פְּשָׁעֵנוּ. עוֹמֵס וְהוּא מְחוֹלָל מִפְּשָׁעֵינוּ. סוֹבֵל עַל שֶׁכֶם חַטֹּאתֵינוּ. סְלִיחָה
מְצָא לַעֲוֹנוֹתֵינוּ. נִרְפָּא לָנוּ בְּחַבּוּרָתוֹ. נֶצַח בְּרִיָּה חֲדָשָׁה עֵת לִבְרֹאתוֹ.
מֵחוּג הַעֲלֵהוּ מִשֵּׂעִיר הַדְלֵהוּ. לְהַשְׁמִיעֵנוּ בְּהַר הַלְּבָנוֹן. שֵׁנִית בְּיַד יִנּוֹן.”

Would the great Jewish religious poet Kether have voiced the above had he not felt that the prophecy of *Isaiah* 53, mirroring the great sufferer of the human race who brings redemption through his vicarious atonement, had been fulfilled in Jesus?

Why is this fact kept from us? Why, it may be asked, is the prophecy of *Isaiah* 53 ignored in the Haftorah* readings in connection with the Pentateuchal lessons? Here is recorded the truest portrait of our Messiah. Receive Him into your heart and your sins will be forgiven by His *Korban.* He was wounded for your transgressions and crushed for your iniquities.

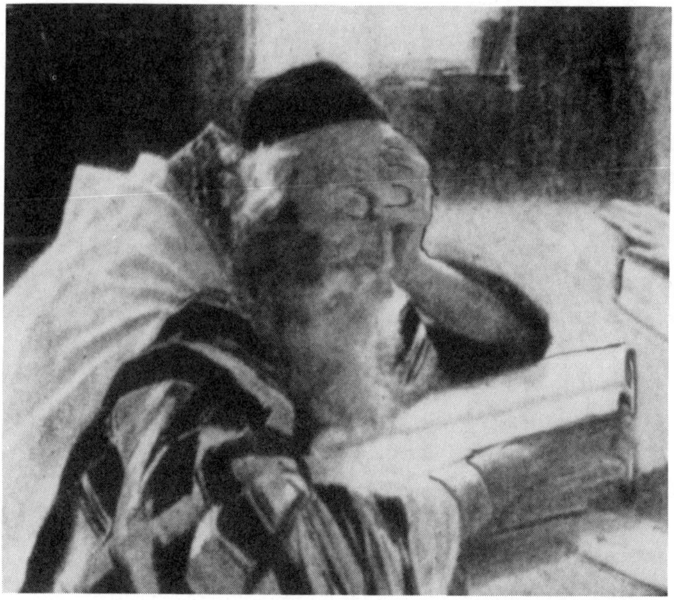

# *Kidush Hashem*

By AGNES WALDSTEIN

When Jesus taught his disciples he rarely used phrases completely new or alien to them, but spoke in terms with which they were familiar, to which he gave an enlarged meaning. He rendered explicit that which had been implicit, and endeavored to unfold more and more of the divine truth contained in the TORAH,* so as to make it available for the perfecting of the religious life.

This is particularly true of the Lord's Prayer (*Matthew* 6:9-13). There is nothing un-Jewish in it. In fact, some rabbis have said that this great prayer is the most Jewish utterance which has come from the mouth of Jesus.

To substantiate this assertion let us consider the first phrase of the Lord's Prayer: HALLOWED BE THY NAME. Its Hebrew equivalent is: *Kidush Hashem.* It is generally taught that this phrase is a reverend bow before the Father in heaven, an acknowledgment of His ruling.

How different it is in Hebrew! *Kidush Hashem* is an awe-inspiring phrase by which a Jew is reminded of the tremendous power of God, of His unfailing judgment, His unfathomable perfection, but not less of His goodness, constant help in the trials of His people, and His faithfulness.

Because of all these implications *Kidush Hashem*, the hallowing of the Name, the unknown Name of God, has also an active meaning. It is the phrase which is used for the death of martyrs. The Jew's duty is to hallow God's Name by dying for it, to give everything and hold back nothing in order that God's Name may be praised. *Kidush Hashem* embodies the greatest demand on the Jew, and the greatest joy which is his in fulfilling it.

Thus when Jesus taught his disciples this prayer, he began with words which to his hearers meant that a demand for their whole being was being made by the Only One who had a right to make such demands. If we place this interpretation upon it, what enormous power and weight the Lord's Prayer receives!

The Jewish meaning of *Kidush Hashem* throws its light also on the requests that follow: THY KINGDOM COME. THY WILL BE DONE, ON EARTH AS IT IS IN HEAVEN.

We are bound to the Kingdom and its King by a loyalty that must prove itself by a preparedness for death. Just as we see soldiers ready to give their lives for their country, so we learn from *Kidush Hashem* that the Kingdom we hope and pray for needs our complete surrender to the One who rules it. His will alone be done, no more ours, for we have made the great sacrifice that is demanded by *Kidush Hashem*.

We can now see that in the Lord's Prayer is suggested something of our cooperation with God, but it is a definitely defined cooperation, the name of which is sacrifice. Only as those who exist no longer for themselves may we put to God requests for our own needs: GIVE US THIS DAY OUR DAILY BREAD; AND FORGIVE US OUR DEBTS, AS WE ALSO HAVE FORGIVEN OUR DEBTORS; AND LEAD US NOT INTO TEMPTATION, BUT DELIVER US FROM EVIL.

If we die for God, He will raise us to a new life in the Spirit, and our prayer for our own needs will no longer be a request that may or may not be granted. It carries in itself the assurance of fulfillment.

God grant that we may be able to hallow His Name!

# GOOD NEWS FROM THE TENACH

By LILLI WOLFF

**DO YOU KNOW?**

God, through His eternal spirit, controlled the men who wrote His Word so that they recorded His thoughts.

*Psalm* 22 is sometimes called "the Psalm of the Cross." The scene of the crucifixion is the picture of the Good Shepherd giving His life for His sheep.

This sacrificial, substitutionary death has been prefigured in every animal sacrifice in Hebrew religious life, the guiltless dying for the guilty sinner.

David wrote this Psalm 1,000 years before the actual event (*Matthew* 27:35-46), and it is important to remember that at that time the world had not even dreamed of death by crucifixion, nor of the Roman Empire. Crucifixion was a Roman means of execution, not Jewish.

PSALM

22 For the Leader; upon Aijeleth ha-Shahar. A Psalm of David.

2 My God, my God, why hast Thou forsaken me,
And art far from my help at the words of my cry?
3 O my God, I call by day, but Thou answerest not;
And at night, and there is no surcease for me.
4 Yet Thou art holy,
O Thou that art enthroned upon the praises of Israel.
5 In Thee did our fathers trust;
They trusted, and Thou didst deliver them.
6 Unto Thee they cried, and escaped;
In Thee did they trust, and were not ashamed.
7 But I am a worm, and no man;
A reproach of men, and despised of the people.
8 All they that see me laugh me to scorn;
They shoot out the lip, they shake the head:
9 'Let him commit himself unto the LORD! let Him rescue him;
Let Him deliver him, seeing He delighteth in him.'

10 For Thou art He that took me out of the womb;
Thou madest me trust when I was upon my mother's breasts.
11 Upon Thee I have been cast from my birth;
Thou art my God from my mother's womb.
12 Be not far from me; for trouble is near;
For there is none to help.
13 Many bulls have encompassed me;
Strong bulls of Bashan have beset me round.
14 They open wide their mouth against me,
As a ravening and a roaring lion.
15 I am poured out like water,
And all my bones are out of joint;
My heart is become like wax;
It is melted in mine inmost parts.
16 My strength is dried up like a potsherd;
And my tongue cleaveth to my throat;
And Thou layest me in the dust of death.
17 For dogs have encompassed me;
A company of evil-doers have inclosed me;
Like a lion, they are at my hands and my feet.
18 I may count all my bones;
They look and gloat over me.
19 They part my garments among them,
And for my vesture do they cast lots.
20 But Thou, O LORD, be not far off;
O Thou my strength, hasten to help me.
21 Deliver my soul from the sword;
Mine only one from the power of the dog.
22 Save me from the lion's mouth;
Yea, from the horns of the wild-oxen do Thou answer me.

23 I will declare Thy name unto my brethren;
In the midst of the congregation will I praise Thee:
24 'Ye that fear the LORD, praise Him;
All ye the seed of Jacob, glorify Him;
And stand in awe of Him, all ye the seed of Israel.
25 For He hath not despised nor abhorred the lowliness of the poor;
Neither hath He hid His face from him;
But when he cried unto Him, He heard.'
26 From Thee cometh my praise in the great congregation;
I will pay my vows before them that fear Him.
27 Let the humble eat and be satisfied;

## DO YOU KNOW?

According to the Word of God, perilous times are coming upon the earth. Bewilderment, perplexity, and fear will grip the hearts of men.

Daniel and Jeremiah spoke of a time of tribulation (*Daniel* 12:1; *Jeremiah* 30:7), "a time of trouble unto Jacob."

The Prophet of whom Moses wrote (*Deuteronomy* 18:15-19), whose Hebrew name is Yeshua-Jesus, said: "For then shall be great tribulation such as was not since the beginning of the world to this time, no, nor ever shall be" (*Matthew* 24:21).

Today the eyes of the world are upon Israel, hemmed in on every side by enemies. Events move rapidly. Jacob's trouble draws near. Surely, it may begin any time.

The question must be: how to escape?

God answers: "Do homage in purity, lest He be angry, and ye perish in the way" (*Psalm* 2:12).

To reject Yeshua-Jesus as Messiah is to meet Him as judge.

DANIEL

utterly to make away many. 45 And
he shall plant the tents of his palace
between the seas and the beauteous
holy mountain; and he shall come to
his end, and none shall help him.
**12** And at that time shall Michael
stand up, the great prince who
standeth for the children of thy
people; and there shall be a time of
trouble, such as never was since there
was a nation even to that same time;
and at that time thy people shall be
delivered, every one that shall be
found written in the book. 2 And many
of them that sleep in the dust of the
earth shall awake, some to everlasting
life, and some to reproaches and
everlasting abhorrence. 3 And they
that are wise shall shine as the brightness
of the firmament; and they that
turn the many to righteousness as the

JEREMIAH 30

6 Ask ye now, and see
Whether a man doth travail with child;
Wherefore do I see every man
With his hands on his loins, as a woman in travail,
And all faces are turned into paleness?
7 Alas! for that day is great,
So that none is like it;
And it is a time of trouble unto Jacob,
But out of it shall he be saved.
8 And it shall come to pass in that day,
Saith the LORD of hosts,
That I will break his yoke from off thy neck,
And will burst thy bands;
And strangers shall no more make him their bondman;

## DEUTERONOMY 18

12 For whosoever doeth these things
is an abomination unto the Lord;
and because of these abominations
the Lord thy God is driving them out
from before thee. 13 Thou shalt be
whole-hearted with the Lord thy God.
14 For these nations, that thou art to
dispossess, hearken unto soothsayers,
and unto diviners; but as for thee, the
Lord thy God hath not suffered thee
so to do. 15 A prophet will the Lord
thy God raise up unto thee, from the
midst of thee, of thy brethren, like
unto me; unto him ye shall hearken;
16 according to all that thou didst desire
of the Lord thy God in Horeb in the
day of the assembly, saying: 'Let
me not hear again the voice of the
Lord my God, neither let me see this
great fire any more, that I die not.'
17 And the Lord said unto me: 'They
have well said that which they have
spoken. 18 I will raise them up a
prophet from among their brethren,
like unto thee; and I will put My
words in his mouth, and he shall
speak unto them all that I shall com-
mand him. 19 And it shall come to pass,
that whosoever will not hearken un-
to My words which he shall speak in
My name, I will require it of him.
20 But the prophet, that shall speak a
word presumptuously in My name,
which I have not commanded him to
speak, or that shall speak in the name
of other gods, that same prophet
shall die.' 21 And if thou say in thy
heart: 'How shall we know the word
which the Lord hath not spoken?'

## PSALM 2

2 Why are the nations in an uproar?
And why do the peoples mutter
in vain?
2 The kings of the earth stand up,
And the rulers take counsel together,
Against the Lord, and against His
anointed:
3 'Let us break their bands asun-
der,
And cast away their cords from us.'

4 He that sitteth in heaven laugheth,
The Lord hath them in derision.
5 Then will He speak unto them in
His wrath,
And affright them in His sore dis-
pleasure:
6 'Truly it is I that have established
My king
Upon Zion, My holy mountain.'

7 I will tell of the decree:
The Lord said unto me: 'Thou
art My son,
This day have I begotten thee.
8 Ask of Me, and I will give the
nations for thine inheritance,
And the ends of the earth for thy
possession.
9 Thou shalt break them with a rod
of iron;
Thou shalt dash them in pieces
like a potter's vessel.'
10 Now therefore, O ye kings, be wise;
Be admonished, ye judges of the
earth.
11 Serve the Lord with fear,
And rejoice with trembling.
12 Do homage in purity, lest He be
angry, and ye perish in the way,
When suddenly His wrath is kindled.

## DO YOU KNOW?

The covenants which God made with the patriarchs: Abraham (*Genesis* 12:1-3), Isaac (*Genesis* 26:4), and Jacob (*Genesis* 28:14), end with the promise of the coming of the Redeemer-Messiah, the One in whom "all the nations of the earth shall be blessed." In His covenant with King David (*II Samuel* 7:12, 13), God promised that this One should be:

(1) of the royal family of David (2) an eternal "seed" (3) ruler over an eternal kingdom (4) builder of an eternal house (dynasty) (5) King upon an eternal throne.

The Prophet Isaiah gives the name of this One who shall sit upon David's throne, "Immanuel" (*Isaiah* 7:14), which Hebrew word means, "God with us."

GENESIS

**12** Now the LORD said unto
Abram: 'Get thee out of thy
country, and from thy kindred, and
from thy father's house, unto the land
that I will show thee. 2And I will make
of thee a great nation, and I will bless
thee, and make thy name great; and be
thou a blessing. 3And I will bless
them that bless thee, and him that
curseth thee will I curse; and in
thee shall all the families of the
earth be blessed.' 4So Abram went,
as the LORD had spoken unto him;
and Lot went with him; and Abram
was seventy and five years old when
he departed out of Haran. 5And
Abram took Sarai his wife, and Lot his
brother's son, and all their substance
that they had gathered, and the souls
that they had gotten in Haran; and
they went forth to go into the land of
Canaan; and into the land of Canaan
they came. 6And Abram passed
through the land unto the place of
Shechem, unto the terebinth of Moreh.
And the Canaanite was then in the

GENESIS

**26** And there was a famine in the
land, beside the first famine that
was in the days of Abraham. And
Isaac went unto Abimelech king of
the Philistines unto Gerar. 2And the
LORD appeared unto him, and said:
'Go not down into Egypt; dwell in
the land which I shall tell thee of.
3Sojourn in this land, and I will be
with thee, and will bless thee; for unto
thee, and unto thy seed, I will give all
these lands, and I will establish the
oath which I swore unto Abraham
thy father; 4and I will multiply thy
seed as the stars of heaven, and will
give unto thy seed all these lands;
and by thy seed shall all the nations of
the earth bless themselves; 5because
that Abraham hearkened to My voice,
and kept My charge, My command-
ments, My statutes, and My laws.'
6And Isaac dwelt in Gerar. 7And
the men of the place asked him of his
wife; and he said: 'She is my sister';
for he feared to say: 'My wife'; 'lest
the men of the place should kill

## GENESIS 28

10 And Jacob went out from Beer-
sheba, and went toward Haran.
11 And he lighted upon the place, and
tarried there all night, because the
sun was set; and he took one of the
stones of the place, and put it under
his head, and lay down in that place
to sleep. 12 And he dreamed, and be-
hold a ladder set up on the earth, and
the top of it reached to heaven; and
behold the angels of God ascending
and descending on it. 13 And, behold,
the LORD stood beside him, and said:
'I am the LORD, the God of Abraham
thy father, and the God of Isaac.
The land whereon thou liest, to thee
will I give it, and to thy seed. 14 And
thy seed shall be as the dust of the
earth, and thou shalt spread abroad
to the west, and to the east, and to the
north, and to the south. And in
thee and in thy seed shall all the
families of the earth be blessed.
15 And, behold, I am with thee, and
will keep thee whithersoever thou
goest, and will bring thee back into this
land; for I will not leave thee, until I
have done that which I have spoken to
thee of.' 16 And Jacob awaked out of
his sleep, and he said: 'Surely the
LORD is in this place; and I knew it
not.' 17 And he was afraid, and said:
'How full of awe is this place! this is
none other than the house of God,
and this is the gate of heaven.' 18 And
Jacob rose up early in the morning,
and took the stone that he had put
under his head, and set it up for a
pillar, and poured oil upon the top of
it. 19 And he called the name of that
place [a]Beth-el, but the name of the
city was Luz at the first. 20 And Jacob
vowed a vow, saying: 'If God will
be with me, and will keep me in this
way that I go, and will give me bread
to eat, and raiment to put on, 21 so

## ISAIAH 7

will I try the LORD.' 13 And he said:
'Hear ye now, O house of David:
Is it a small thing for you to weary
men, that ye will weary my God
also? 14 Therefore the Lord Himself
shall give you a sign: behold, the
young woman shall conceive, and
bear a son, and shall call his name
[a]Immanuel. 15 Curd and honey shall
he eat, when he knoweth to refuse
the evil, and choose the good. 16 Yea,
before the child shall know to refuse
the evil, and choose the good, the
land whose two kings thou hast a
horror of shall be forsaken. 17 The
LORD shall bring upon thee, and upon
thy people, and upon thy father's
house, days that have not come, from
the day that Ephraim departed from
Judah; even the king of Assyria.'

18 And it shall come to pass in that day,
That the LORD shall hiss for the fly
That is in the uttermost part of
the rivers of Egypt,
And for the bee that is in the land
of Assyria.
19 And they shall come, and shall rest
all of them
In the rugged valleys, and in the
holes of the rocks,
And upon all thorns, and upon all
brambles.

20 In that day shall the Lord shave
with a razor that is hired in the parts
beyond the River, even with the king
of Assyria, the head and the hair of
the feet; and it shall also sweep away
the beard.

21 And it shall come to pass in that
day, that a man shall rear a young
cow, and two sheep; 22 and it shall come
to pass, for the abundance of milk
that they shall give, he shall eat curd;
for curd and honey shall every one eat
that is left in the midst of the land.

23 And it shall come to pass in that
day, that every place, where there

## DO YOU KNOW?

Over 700 years before it came to pass, Micah (the prophet who lived during the reigns of Jothan, Ahaz, Hezekiah—kings of Judah), wrote that the Messiah would be born in Bethlehem of Judea (*Micah* 5:1).

He said that this "ruler in Israel" had been "from of old, from ancient days," the eternal Sovereign of the universe.

The Jewish historian, Matthew, writing to Jews confirmed the express fulfillment of these words (*Matthew* 2:1-6).

Isaiah, the prophet of Judah, wrote of the coming of the Messiah. Among other things he said that a child would be born; also his names were mentioned (*Isaiah* 9:5-6).

MICAH

5 But thou, Beth-lehem Ephrathah,
Which art little to be among the thousands of Judah,
Out of thee shall one come forth unto Me that is to be ruler in Israel;

ISAIAH

9 The people that walked in darkness
Have seen a great light;
They that dwelt in the land of the shadow of death,
Upon them hath the light shined.
2 Thou hast multiplied the nation,
Thou hast increased their joy;
They joy before Thee according to the joy in harvest,
As men rejoice when they divide the spoil.
3 For the yoke of his burden,
And the staff of his shoulder,
The rod of his oppressor,
Thou hast broken as in the day of Midian.

ISAIAH 9

4 For every boot stamped with fierceness,
And every cloak rolled in blood,
Shall even be for burning, for fuel of fire.
5 **For a child is born unto us,**
**A son is given unto us;**
**And the government is upon his shoulder;**
And his name is called
[a] Pele-joez-el-gibbor-
Abi-ad-sar-shalom;
6 That the government may be increased,
And of peace there be no end,
Upon the throne of David, and upon his kingdom,
To establish it, and to uphold it
Through justice and through righteousness
From henceforth even for ever.
The zeal of the LORD of hosts doth perform this.

[a] That is, *Wonderful in counsel is God the Mighty, the Everlasting Father, the Ruler of peace.*

# *Is the New Testament Anti-Semitic?*

By VICTOR BUKSBAZEN

The New Testament is a book which to millions of people reveals God's love for all men. In recent years this book has been attacked by some Jewish leaders as responsible for Christian hostility to the Jews. Some even demanded that the New Testament be corrected and the so-called anti-Semitic statements be removed.

Jewish opposition to the New Testament has a history which goes back to the very beginning of the Christian movement. Some of the ancient Rabbis have coined a pun on the Greek word for the Gospel, "Evangelion," and called it in Hebrew "avon Gillion"— "The scroll of sin." Others have perverted the Hebrew name of Jesus, "Yeshua," into "Yeshu," the letters of which comprise the initials of the words, "Yemach shemo vezichro"—"May his name be obliterated and forgotten."

The original hostility to Jesus was based on the charge that Jesus committed blasphemy:

> THIS WAS WHY THE JEWS SOUGHT ALL THE MORE TO KILL HIM, BECAUSE HE NOT ONLY BROKE THE SABBATH BUT ALSO CALLED GOD HIS FATHER, MAKING HIMSELF EQUAL WITH GOD (*John* 5:18).

To the old charges against the New Testament, new ones were added later. Assertions were made that the New Testament account of the crucifixion casts the Jews in the role of "Christkillers," thus fostering "Christian anti-Semitism."

Another accusation was made that the New Testament contains a number of anti-Semitic passages. Before we proceed further, it is necessary to answer two basic questions: (1) Who were the authors of the New Testament? (2) Were they reliable and trustworthy witnesses?

It should be remembered that the first disciples and followers of Jesus were all Jews, most of them Galileans, a simple and patriotic people who often rebelled against their Roman oppressors. They shared the trials and tribulations of their Jewish countrymen, and with them hoped for a speedy redemption from their oppressors and for the coming of the Messiah to deliver them.

The figure around whose life and message the New Testament is centered was Jesus, the Man from Galilee, a descendant of the house of David (*Matthew* chapter 1; *Luke* 3:23-38). He lived a holy and blameless life, and was the only person in history who could challenge his opponents with the question, "Which of you convicts me of sin?" (*John* 8:46).

An unbiased reader of the New Testament will soon discover that this is a book which breathes a spirit of love and compassion for all men, and tender feelings for the Jewish people, the kinsmen of Jesus.

Like the prophets of the TENACH,* Jesus called his people to repentance and to return to God. He grieved over Israel's disobedience to God and their unbelief. On one occasion Jesus wept over Jerusalem and lamented in these words:

> O JERUSALEM, JERUSALEM, KILLING THE PROPHETS AND STONING THOSE WHO ARE SENT TO YOU! HOW OFTEN WOULD I HAVE GATHERED YOUR CHILDREN TOGETHER AS A HEN GATHERS HER BROOD UNDER HER WINGS, AND YOU WOULD NOT! BEHOLD, YOUR HOUSE IS FORSAKEN AND DESOLATE (*Matthew* 23:37-38).

Some forty years later his words came true. Jerusalem became desolate, and the Holy Temple was razed by the Romans.

His love for Israel and his faith in their high calling to be a light to the nations were beyond question. Speaking to a Samaritan woman at the well in Sychar (modern Nablus), Jesus pronounced these timeless words: "You worship what you do not know; we worship what we know, for salvation is from the Jews" (*John* 4:22).

His words of rebuke were similar to those of a prophet, a lover of his people, and not of an enemy. This is also true of the famous Saul-Paul who was once an ardent Pharisee and persecuted the Jewish believers in Jesus. Saul-Paul gave us a glimpse into his own heart in these words: "Brethren, my heart's desire and prayer to God for them is that they might be saved" (*Romans* 10:1).

His faith in the election of Israel was unshakable in spite of their disobedience to God. "I ask, then, has God rejected his people? By no means! I myself am an Israelite, a descendant of Abraham, a member of the tribe of Benjamin" (*Romans* 11:1).

Saul-Paul added this affirmation of Israel's final redemption and glorious destiny: "And so all Israel will be saved" (*Romans* 11:26).

The apostles were loyal sons of Israel and, like the prophets of old, burned with a holy fire of indignation against disobedience to God, and possessed an unquenchable desire that Israel be saved.

Any historical document is only as trustworthy as its author. The matchless nobility of character of Jesus and his disciples, and their absolute dedication to the truth, are a guarantee of the trustworthiness of the New Testament. Since the authors of the New Testament were men of high moral and spiritual integrity, we must assume that what they have recorded is of the highest order of truth, God's truth. If we cannot trust the New Testament, neither can we trust any historical record. All history then becomes a deception and a delusion. (See "The Bible—An Historical Document," p. 4.)

Some statements in the New Testament may sound harsh to the casual or superficial reader, especially when taken out of the context of time and circumstances. Even the disciples of Jesus took exception to some of his sayings. For instance, when he asserted:

> I AM THE LIVING BREAD WHICH CAME DOWN FROM HEAVEN; IF ANY ONE EATS OF THIS BREAD, HE WILL LIVE FOREVER; AND THE BREAD WHICH I SHALL GIVE FOR THE LIFE OF THE WORLD IS MY FLESH (*John* 6:51).

We read that from that moment many of his disciples drew back and walked with him no more (*John* 6:52-66).

The sayings of Jesus always provoked the opposition and antagonism of those who were carnally minded and not attuned spiritually to his person and message. However, this is also true of the TENACH.* Long before the days of Jesus we find that the people equally objected to the prophets because they did not like to listen to things which interfered with their selfish ways or made demands on their moral or spiritual life. Isaiah accurately described the attitudes of Israel's leaders to the prophets of his own time:

> THAT SAY TO THE SEERS: "SEE NOT,"
> AND TO THE PROPHETS: "PROPHESY NOT UNTO US RIGHT THINGS,
> SPEAK UNTO US SMOOTH THINGS, PROPHESY DELUSIONS" (*Isaiah* 30:10).

Was the Prophet Isaiah an anti-Semite because he called the leaders of his time, "Rulers of Sodom," and his kinsmen, "Ye people of Gomorrah"? (*Isaiah* 1:10) Of course not! The prophets were impelled by God and their overburdened hearts to speak the truth as they saw it. The same was true of Jesus and his disciples who taught in the line of the prophetic tradition. Their castigation had one purpose: repentance and spiritual rebirth. This kind of teaching has always provoked resentment.

There were other reasons for the opposition of the religious leadership to Jesus. They objected to his castigation of the establishment: the Temple priests, the Scribes, the Pharisees, and the elders.

Another and even more basic reason for their hostility was, as we have already observed, his extraordinary claim to be the Son of God. In the eyes of his opponents this was blasphemy worthy of death.

After Jesus healed a paralytic on the Sabbath Day, we read:

> THIS WAS WHY THE JEWS SOUGHT ALL THE MORE TO KILL HIM, BECAUSE HE NOT ONLY BROKE THE SABBATH BUT ALSO CALLED GOD HIS FATHER, MAKING HIMSELF EQUAL WITH GOD (*John* 5:18).

The oft misunderstood use of the term "the Jews" in the Gospel of John requires a word of explanation. Quite frequently it is used collectively for the organized opposition to Jesus, but it is also employed to describe the inhabitants of Jerusalem and Judea.

However, the expression, "the Jews," is also used in a positive and favorable sense as when Jesus says to a Samaritan woman, "Salvation is from the Jews" (*John* 4:22).

Jesus himself was called "a Jew" by the Samaritan woman without any objection or denial on his part.

Sometimes the designation "the Jews" is also applied to those people who admired Jesus and followed him (*John* 11:45; 12:11).

It is interesting to note that in the Book of Revelation, generally attributed to the Apostle John, is a vision of the end times and of the redeemed of all nations in heaven. Among these are a hundred and forty-four thousand representing the twelve tribes of Israel:

> AND I HEARD THE NUMBER OF THE SEALED, A HUNDRED AND FORTY-FOUR THOUSAND SEALED, OUT OF EVERY TRIBE OF THE SONS OF ISRAEL ... AFTER THIS I LOOKED, AND BEHOLD, A

> GREAT MULTITUDE WHICH NO MAN COULD NUMBER, FROM EVERY NATION, FROM ALL TRIBES AND PEOPLES AND TONGUES, STANDING BEFORE THE THRONE AND BEFORE THE LAMB, CLOTHED IN WHITE ROBES, WITH PALM BRANCHES IN THEIR HANDS (*Revelation* 7:4, 9).

Here is a redeemed remnant of Israel which lives on till the end of time, and is assigned a foremost place of honor among the blessed of all nations. This is hardly the sentiment of an anti-Semite. It is more in keeping with Jeremiah's prophecy of the indestructibility of Israel (*Jeremiah* 31:35-37).

In the past the Gospel of John was considered the most Hellenistic of all the Gospels. New Testament scholars now commonly assume that it is the most Jewish Gospel. Like the Qumran writings, with which it has a number of similarities, it is also a document of protest against the Temple priesthood and the official religious establishment. When John refers to "the Jews" he frequently means the organized opposition to Jesus and his followers, arising primarily from the religious leaders.

The Gospel of John was written after the fall of Jerusalem, predicted by Jesus (*Matthew* 23:37-38), when the Synagogue changed its liturgy to make it impossible for Jewish believers in Jesus to stay inside the community. John took his place alongside this persecuted minority around the year 80-90 C.E., being forced out of the Jewish community of which they had hitherto been an integral part.

This was the historical setting of John's Gospel. It was a time when the Synagogue persecuted the young Church in Jerusalem. John's Gospel tells of an embattled and harassed minority, torn between love for its people and loyalty to Jesus, the Messiah.

In the 23rd chapter of Matthew Jesus pronounced a series of prophetic woes, similar to Isaiah's, not against the teaching of the Pharisees but against the insincerity of some of them (by no means all). Jesus distinctly approved of many of their teachings, but warned his disciples against their ways and practices, "for they preach, but do not practice" (*Matthew* 23:3).

He followed this with some grave accusations: "They bind heavy burdens, hard to bear, and lay them on men's shoulders; but they themselves will not move them with their finger" (*Matthew* 23:4).

Jesus continued that the Pharisees love ostentatious prominence, to be seated in the place of honor in the synagogues, and to be called Rabbi or Master (verses 5-12).

Jesus then pronounced a series of woes against the Scribes and Pharisees, calling them hypocrites, for they devour widows' houses and for a pretense make long prayers (verse 14).

He called them blind guides who strain out a gnat and swallow a camel (verse 24).

If one is to charge Jesus with being unkind to the Pharisees, what must we say about prophets like Isaiah who castigated mercilessly the leaders of his people in even more scathing words: "Woe unto them that call evil good, and good evil . . . Woe unto them that are wise in their own eyes . . . That justify the wicked for a reward . . ." (*Isaiah* 5:20-23).

What about Jeremiah's lament: "Concerning the prophets. My heart within me is broken . . . For both prophet and priest are ungodly . . ." (*Jeremiah* 23:9, 11).

The harsh condemnations of false prophets, priests, and unfaithful shepherds were far more frequent in the TENACH* than in the New Testament. Should we therefore call the prophets of the TENACH* anti-Semites? They spoke as the Spirit of God moved them, even as Jesus and his disciples did.

Much has been made by Jew-haters of every generation of the conduct of the Jerusalem crowd and their leaders when Jesus stood before Pontius Pilate for final sentencing. The Gospels record (*Matthew* 27:15-25; *Mark* 15:7-15; *Luke* 23:13-24) how the crowd incited by the priests demanded from Pilate that he set free Barabbas and crucify Jesus:

> LET HIM BE CRUCIFIED . . . HIS BLOOD BE ON US AND ON OUR CHILDREN (*Matthew* 27:22, 25).

Many misguided Christians have argued that by these words of the Jerusalem mob and their leaders the Jews have called down upon themselves and upon Jews of all generations the wrath of God, and consequently deserve to be persecuted and punished.

One of the obsessive fears of many Jewish people is their belief that the crucifixion account singles them out as a nation of "Christkillers," and that this is the underlying cause of anti-Semitism.

The pagans of the pre-Christian era hated the Jews, persecuted them, and often resorted to pogroms centuries before Jesus. They found excuses for their wicked acts, such as: Jews were atheists because they worshiped an invisible God. Or: Jews were lazy because they refused to work on the Sabbath.

Should we condemn all Greeks of every generation for the judicial murder of Socrates, committed by some of the foolish leaders of Athens in the fourth century B.C.E.?

Should we hold every Russian responsible for the bloody murders of Stalin, or all the Germans for the heinous deeds of the madman Hitler and his henchmen?

For every Jew who shouted "Let him be crucified," there were many devout Jewish men and women who followed Jesus to the cross weeping.

What does the New Testament really teach about the meaning of the crucifixion of Jesus? Does it hold up the Jews for scorn or contempt? Indeed not! The meaning of the cross is summed up by the Apostle John in these words: "For God so loved the world that he gave his only Son, that whoever believes in Him should not perish but have eternal life" (*John* 3:16).

The whole emphasis of the New Testament is not on men, but on God Himself and His eternal purpose of reconciling the world to Himself through the sacrifice of His Son.

When Jews speak of anti-Semitism in the New Testament, this merely indicates that they are reading into it their own distorted perspectives, or their own unfortunate experiences through the centuries among so-called Christians.

Those who blame the Jews for the crucifixion have completely missed the significance of the cross.

# BLESSED BE EGYPT?

By DANIEL FUCHS

"Blessed be Egypt, My people . . ." This prophecy found in *Isaiah* 19:25 is one of the most startling promises in the TENACH.* "Blessed be Egypt?" From the birth of the nation of Israel until today there has never been a nation that persisted so long and so violently in persecuting the Jews.

It is true that Germany in modern times sought to destroy the nation, but the modern anti-Semitism of Hitler is short-lived in comparison to the 3,500 years from Pharaoh to Sadat. Besides, Hitler admitted that he was just inserting a page into the history that Pharaoh began to write.

How could God who promised to Abram, "I will bless them that bless thee and curse him that curseth thee" ever bless Egypt at all? The Lord not only extended His blessing to Egypt, but called them "My people." This seems to be the most incredible prophecy in the Scriptures.

It is even more difficult to think that in our day we might be seeing the ground-work laid for the fulfillment of this prophecy. A few years ago one would matriculate into an asylum by even mentioning the remote possibility that Sadat would ever visit Jerusalem while a single Jew still lived. But look what has happened! Anwar Sadat and Menachem Begin have spoken with each other, and the prospect of face-to-face negotiations between Israel and Egypt is not only a possibility but a reality. It seems that *Isaiah* 19 is highly significant.

At this point it is very important that I make my position clear. I am not stating that Sadat's visit to Jerusalem is the beginning of the fulfillment of *Isaiah* 19. However, it may be the initial act in this drama. One thing we are sure of, the Scriptures clearly teach that Israel and Egypt will one day be allies. Not only that, but Egypt will worship the God of Abraham, Isaac, and Jacob!

> IN THAT DAY THERE SHALL BE FIVE CITIES IN THE LAND OF EGYPT THAT SPEAK THE LANGUAGE OF CANAAN, AND SWEAR TO THE LORD OF HOSTS . . . IN THAT DAY SHALL THERE BE AN ALTAR TO THE LORD IN THE MIDST OF THE LAND OF EGYPT, AND A PILLAR AT THE BORDER THEREOF TO THE LORD. AND IT SHALL BE FOR A SIGN AND FOR A WITNESS UNTO THE LORD OF HOSTS IN THE LAND OF EGYPT . . .
>
> IN THAT DAY THERE SHALL BE A HIGHWAY OUT OF EGYPT TO ASSYRIA, AND THE ASSYRIAN SHALL COME INTO EGYPT, AND THE EGYPTIANS INTO ASSYRIA; AND THE EGYPTIANS SHALL WORSHIP WITH THE ASSYRIANS.
>
> IN THAT DAY SHALL ISRAEL BE THE THIRD WITH EGYPT AND WITH ASSYRIA, A BLESSING IN THE MIDST OF THE EARTH; FOR THAT THE LORD OF HOSTS HATH BLESSED HIM, SAYING: "BLESSED BE EGYPT MY PEOPLE AND ASSYRIA THE WORK OF MY HANDS, AND ISRAEL MINE INHERITANCE" (*Isaiah* 19:18-25).

What an amazing prophecy! I must repeat my question. How could God who promised to Abram, "I will bless them that bless thee, and curse him that curseth thee" ever bless Egypt at all?

The answer is in the same verse of the Abrahamic Covenant.

God promised, "I will bless them that bless thee." Three times Egypt was a blessing to the people of God. We may have forgotten these three acts of blessing but God remembers!

We have castigated all the Pharaohs because of the Pharaoh "who knew not Joseph" (*Exodus* 1:8). However, when Joseph's brothers sold him as a slave there was a Pharaoh that made him a ruler (*Genesis* 41:40). Joseph was God's instrument in preserving Israel's family, and Pharaoh helped! It was in Egypt that the family of God grew and was welded into a nation.

Why was it necessary for God to bring the chosen family into the land of Egypt? Secular history tells us of the disgusting conditions of the so-called "Canaanitish" civilization. As the family of Israel multiplied it would have been virtually impossible to keep out the corrupting influence of the Canaanites. The family would be assimilated. The Egyptian civilization was the highest of its day. No finer home could be found than the land of Goshen near the Nile River. God brought Joseph to this land. Joseph became so famous that Pharaoh was delighted to welcome Jacob and his children and to give them the best of the land.

When Jacob and his family went down into Egypt they numbered only seventy people. They were too few to attempt to take possession of the Promised Land. Time and opportunity must be provided for numerical growth. The original seventy grew into a nation of at least two million people.

Twelve hundred years later two of Alexander the Great's generals, Seleucus and Ptolemy, fought for Israel and finally Ptolemy won and once more Israel was ruled by Egypt. For a little more than a century Israel continued under the mild rule of the Ptolemies.

One result of the union between Egypt and Israel was that the Jews became numerous, wealthy, and influential in Alexandria, the chief seaport of the Mediterranean. As Greek was the language of commerce and civilization, it soon became the language of Jews everywhere, except in Israel where a dialect arose blending the old Hebrew with Chaldee and Syriac words.

The lessons were still read in the synagogue from the ancient Hebrew text, but the people couldn't understand it. It had to be interpreted.

In Egypt, among the Jews of the Dispersion, a demand grew for the sacred writings in the Greek language. The names of the translators are not commonly known, but a tradition that there were seventy men gave to the translation the name *Septuagint* from the Latin *septuaginta* "seventy." The version was make between 285 and 245 B.C.E. It was widely welcomed by the Jews of the Dispersion; and now, because it was in Greek, was studied by the Greeks themselves.

It was in Egypt that the Hebrew Scriptures were made available for the entire world. The most important historical event of the inter-testament period was not the wars of Alexander's generals, not the rise of Rome, but the translation of God's Word so that all could read and understand. This was accomplished in Egypt. What a blessing this was to the Jews and to the world! God said, "I will bless them that bless thee."

Two and a half centuries later Israel was ruled by an Edomite usurper, Herod. Late in his reign a Child was born in Bethlehem of Judea.

> NOW WHEN JESUS WAS BORN IN BETHLEHEM OF JUDEA IN THE DAYS OF HEROD THE KING, BEHOLD, WISE MEN FROM THE EAST CAME TO JERUSALEM, SAYING, "WHERE IS HE WHO HAS BEEN BORN KING OF THE JEWS? FOR WE HAVE SEEN HIS STAR IN THE EAST, AND HAVE COME TO WORSHIP HIM" (*Matthew* 2:1-3).

Herod wanted to slay the Child, but an angel warned Joseph:

> "RISE, TAKE THE CHILD AND HIS MOTHER, AND FLEE TO EGYPT, AND REMAIN THERE TILL I TELL YOU; FOR HEROD IS ABOUT TO SEARCH FOR THE CHILD, TO DESTROY HIM." AND HE ROSE AND TOOK THE CHILD AND HIS MOTHER BY NIGHT, AND DEPARTED TO EGYPT (*Matthew* 2:13-14).

This was the third time that God used Egypt for His purpose. Perhaps Sadat's visit is the fourth.

און דער שׂטן האָט אַ דריט מאָל אויסגערעכנט אַלע שלעכטע מעשׂים פֿון דעם ווינדיקן מענטשן.

און דאָס בת־קול האָט געזאָגט: „גיי אַוועק פֿון דאַנען; די ווינדיקע קאָנען ניט אַרײַנקומען אין מלכות־שמים.“

און ס'האָט געענטפֿערט דער בעל־עבֿירהניק: „דײַן קול הער איך; דײַן פּנים אָבער זע איך ניט, און דײַן נאָמען ווייס איך ניט.“

און דאָס בת־קול האָט געענטפֿערט: „איך בין יוחנן, דער תּלמיד וועמען ישוע האָט ליב געהאַט.“

דערויף האָט זיך דערפֿרייט דער ווינדיקער, און געזאָגט: „דו קאָנסט מיר ניט פֿאַרווערן אַרײַנצוקומען. שמעון בר־יונה און דוד המלך וואָלטן מיך אַרײַנגעלאָזט, מחמת שמעון ווייסט גאָטס גרויסע גוטסקייט, און דוד המלך – די מענטשלעכע שוואַכקייט, דו אָבער וועסט מיך אַרײַנלאָזן, מחמת דו פֿאַרמאָגסט אַ סך ליבשאַפֿט. האָסטו ניט בפֿירוש געשריבן אין דײַן ספֿר, אַז גאָט איז ליבשאַפֿט, און אַז דער, וואָס האָט ניט ליב זײַן ברודער, קען ניט גאָט? [יוחנן א׳, ד, 16, 20]. ווי קענסטו מיך אָפּשטויסן פֿון דיר?“

און באותו־רגע האָבן זיך געעפֿנט די טויערן, און יוחנן האָט אַרומגענומען דעם בעל־תּשובה, און האָט אים אַרײַנגעלאָזט אין מלכות־שמים.

„דערמאָנסט זיך ווי דער האָן האָט געקרייַט, און דו האָסט פֿאַר ווייטיק זיך ביטער צעוויינט? אַזוי בין איך אויך. דו קאָנסט מיך ניט פֿאַרשטויסן!"

און ס'איז אַ ווײַלע שטיל געוואָרן.

האָט געוואַרט אַ ביסל דער זינדיקער, און האָט באַלד אָנגעהויבן ווידער קלאַפּן און בעטן מע זאָל אים אַרײַנלאָזן. און פֿון הינטער די טויערן האָט זיך דערהערט אַ צווייט קול, וואָס האָט געזאָגט: „ווער איז דער דאָזיקער מענטש?"

און ווידער האָט זיך אַרײַנגעמישט דער שָׂטן, און האָט איבערגעחַזרט אַלע שלעכטע מַעֲשׂים פֿון דעם זינדיקן.

און דאָס בַּת־קול פֿון הינטער די טויערן האָט געזאָגט: „גיי אַוועק פֿון דאַנען; אַזעלכע זינדיקע מענטשן קאָנען ניט לעבן צוזאַמען מיט די צַדיקים אין מַלכות־שָׁמַיִם."

און דער זינדיקער האָט געזאָגט: „איך הער אַ קול, אָבער איך זע ניט דאָס פָּנים, און דעם נאָמען פֿון דעם, וואָס רעדט צו מיר, ווייס איך ניט."

האָט דאָס בַּת־קול געענטפֿערט: „איך בין דָוִד הַמֶלֶך."

דער זינדיקער האָט אָבער ניט אָפּגעטרויטן, נאָר האָט גענומען זיך בעטן:

„האָב רַחמָנות אויף מיר, דָוִד הַמֶלֶך! באַרעכן די גרויסקייט און דעם חֶסֶד פֿון בּוֹרא, אויך די שוואַכקייט און זינדיקייט פֿון דעם מענטשן. דערמאָן דיך אָן זיך. גאָט האָט דיך ליב געהאַט, און האָט דײַן נאָמען גרויס געמאַכט; פֿאַר אַ קֵיסר האָט ער דיך געמאַכט, און אַלץ האָסטו געהאַט: מלוכה און כָּבוד, ווײַבער און קינדער – און פֿון דײַן דאַך האָסטו געזען דאָס שיינע ווײַב פֿון אַן אָרימען מענטשן, און תֵּיכּף האָט זיך די תַּאווה אין דיר צעשפּילט, און דו האָסט גענומען אוּרִיָהס ווײַב, און אים אַלײן האָסטו געהַרגעט מיטן שווערד פֿון עַמוֹן. דו, אַ נָגִיד, האָסט אָפּגענומען בײַם אֶביוֹן זײַן לעצט שעפּעלע, און אים אַלײן האָסטו אומגעבראַכט – איך האָב אויך אַזוי געטאָן. און דו האָסט דערנאָך תּשובה געטאָן, און געזאָגט: „כִּי פְשָׁעַי אֲנִי אֵדָע וְחַטָאתִי נֶגְדִי תָמִיד – וואָרים איך ווייס מײַנע פֿאַרברעכן, און מײַן חֶטא איז תָּמיד פֿאַר מיר" [תּהִלים נ"א, 5]. אַזוי בין איך אויך. דו קאָנסט מיר ניט ווערן אַרײַנצוקומען."

און שטיל איז געוואָרן דָוִד הַמֶלֶכס שטים.

אָבער די טויערן פֿון מַלכות־שָׁמַיִם זענען נאָך אַלץ פֿאַרמאַכט געווען.

האָט געוואַרט אַ ביסל דער זינדיקער, און האָט באַלד ווידער גענומען קלאַפּן און בעטן מע זאָל אים אַרײַנלאָזן.

האָט זיך אַ דריט בַּת־קול דערהערט, וואָס האָט געזאָגט: „ווער איז דער דאָזיקער מענטש? און ווי האָט ער אָפּגעלעבט זײַן לעבן אויף דער ערד?"

# דער בעל=תשובה

## פון ליעוו טאָלסטאָי

האָט אָפּגעלעבט אויף דער וועלט אַ מענטש זיבעציק יאָר און האָט די גאַנצע זיבעציק יאָר אָפּגעלעבט אין זינד. און עס איז קראַנק געוואָרן דער דאָזיקער מענטש, און ער האָט נאָך אַלץ קיין תשובה ניט געטאָן. נאָר אַ שָׁעה פאַר זיין טויט, האָט ער זיך צעוויינט, און מיט טרערן אין די אויגן אויסגערופן: „רַחמָנותדיקער האַר! זיי מיר מוחל, ווי דו האָסט מוחל געווען דעם גַזלן אויף דער תְּלִיה." און ווי נאָר ער האָט אַרויסגעזאָגט די דאָזיקע ווערטער – איז זיין נשָמה אַרויסגעפלויגן פון זיין גוף. און די נשָמה פון דעם בַּעל־עֲבֵירֶהניק האָט ליב באַקומען גאָט, האָט אָנגעהויבן גלויבן אין זיין גרויס חֶסֶד, און איז געקומען צו די טויערן פון מַלכות־שָׁמַיִם.

און דער זינדיקער האָט אָנגעקלאַפּט אין די טויערן, און געבעטן מע זאָל אים אַרייַנלאָזן. און סע האָט זיך דערהערט אַ בַּת־קול פון הינטער די טויערן: „וואָס פאַר אַ מענטש קלאַפּט דאָ? און וואָס פאַר אַ מַעשׂים האָט ער געטאָן אין די טעג פון זיין לעבן?"

און דער שָׂטן האָט זיך געשטעלט פאַרן בֵּית־דין שֶׁל מַעלה, און האָט אויסגערעכנט אַלע עֲבֵירות פון דעם זינדיקן.

און דאָס בַּת־קול פון הינטער די טויערן האָט געזאָגט: „דער מענטש פון זינד קאָן ניט אַרייַנקומען אַהער; גיי אַוועק פון דאַנען."

און דער מענטש האָט ווידער געזאָגט: „איך הער אַ קול, אָבער איך זע ניט דאָס פָּנים, און דעם נאָמען פון דעם, וואָס רעדט צו מיר, ווייס איך ניט."

האָט דאָס בַּת־קול געענטפערט: „איך בין שִׁמעון בַּר־יונָה."

און דער זינדיקער האָט געזאָגט: „האָב רַחמָנות אויף מיר, שִׁמעון בַּר־יונָה. באַרעכן די גרויסקייט און דעם חֶסֶד פון בורא, אויך די שוואַכקייט און זינדיקייט פון דעם מענטשן. ביסטו ניט געווען איינער פון יֵשוּעס תַּלמידים, וואָס האָסט מיט דיינע אייגענע אויערן זיך צוגעהערט צו זיין געטלעכער תּורה, און זיך צוגעקוקט צו זיין הייליק לעבן? טוסטו זיך ניט דערמאָנען אָן דער צייט, ווען ער האָט געליטן די גרעסטע יסורים, און דו האָסט זיך פון אים אָפּגעטרייסלט? געדענקסט ווי דו האָסט זיך געשוואוירן, אַז דו וועסט אים קיינמאָל ניט פאַרלײַקענען, אַפילו אויב דיר זאָל אויסקומען צו באַצאָלן דערפאַר מיטן לעבן? און דעראֶמתן אָבער האָסו אים דריי מאָל פאַרלייקנט."

# The New Covenant

By J. H. HUNTING

At various times in mankind's history God has made no less than eight covenants with selected members of the human race.

The first, the Edenic, was made with our first ancestor, Adam. The Edenic covenant gave Adam dominion over all living creatures (*Genesis* 1:28-30).

The second, usually called the Adamic, was made with Adam and Eve after they had sinned. This covenant gives the first promise of the Seed of the woman as the Redeemer of mankind who will bruise the serpent's head (*Genesis* 3:13-15).

The third was made with Noah following the great Deluge when God destroyed life on this planet with the exception of those preserved in the Ark (*Genesis* chapter 9).

The fourth was made with Abraham, the ancestor of the Hebrew people, in which the Eternal promised universal blessing through Abraham's seed. The Hebrew nation is to be the channel through which God will ultimately achieve this (*Genesis* 12:1-3).

The fifth covenant was made with Moses at Mount Sinai, and is known as the Law of Moses. This covenant provided a code of laws that set the Hebrews apart from all other peoples (*Exodus* chapters 19 and 20).

The sixth was also made with Moses at Mount Sinai and is called the Palestinian or Canaanitish covenant, and concerned the promise of the land of Canaan as the divinely appointed homeland for the Hebrews (*Deuteronomy* chapters 28 to 30).

The seventh was made with David when God promised that he and his seed would rule over the kingdom. An important aspect of this covenant is that the kingdom and throne of David would be established forever (*II Samuel* 7:16).

Some of the covenants were conditional. For instance, the Lord introduced the Law with these words, "Now therefore, if ye will hearken unto My voice indeed, and keep My covenant . . ." (*Exodus* 19:5).

While the promise of Canaan was unconditional, Israel's continued occupancy depended upon obedience. "And it shall come to pass, if thou shalt hearken diligently unto the voice of the Lord thy God . . ." (*Deuteronomy* 28:1).

On the other hand, no conditions accompanied the covenant that God made with Abraham. Indeed, He confirmed His covenant to Abraham because of his obedience. "And in thy seed shall all the nations of the earth be blessed; because thou hast hearkened to My voice" (*Genesis* 22:18).

The eighth and last of God's covenants with mankind is called the New Covenant. This covenant was promised to Israel by Jeremiah with the words, "Behold, the days come, saith the Lord, that I will make a new covenant with the house of Israel, and with the house of Judah" (*Jeremiah* 31:31-34).

The promise of a new covenant was made when Israel and Judah had sinned against God. Over the centuries Israel lapsed into a life of self-will and disobedience, until the northern kingdom was uprooted and began the long dispersion. The tribe of Judah followed the other tribes into dispersion about 150 years later, and it was at that time, when the covenant which God had made with them on Mount Sinai was in tatters, that "The Lord, the God of their fathers, sent to them by His messengers, sending betimes and often; because He had compassion on His people, and on His dwelling place; but they mocked the messengers of God, and despised His words, and scoffed at His prophets, until the wrath of the Lord arose against His people, till there was no remedy" (*II Chronicles* 36:15-16).

It was in this desperate situation that God had a plan that could not fail to accomplish His purpose in bringing about the ultimate restoration of His covenant people. This plan was in no way associated with the previous covenants which had been so abused. God did not abandon Israel and Judah, and the New Covenant was to be unconditional because it was to depend totally upon God and His faithfulness to fulfill His promise. It was to be introduced at some future date which was unspecified, and it would be a "new" covenant.

There would be a new individual relationship with God instead of implicit obedience to numerous precepts. "I will put My law in their inward parts, and in their heart will I write it; and I will be their God, and they shall be My people" (*Jeremiah* 31:33).

This covenant would change the lives and attitudes of the people, "And they shall teach no more every man his neighbor, and every man his brother, saying: 'Know the Lord'; for they shall all know Me, from the least of them unto the greatest of them" (31:34).

And there would be reconciliation, "For I will forgive their iniquity, and their sin will I remember no more."

Has the promise of the New Covenant been repealed, modified or annulled? Some five hundred years after Jeremiah's prophecy, a small group of men met in Jerusalem. It was the 14th of *Nisan*,* and, according to the commandment of Moses, they partook of the Passover at evening. In the main they were a rugged and strange group of men who arranged themselves at the low Seder* table. Some were fishermen from Galilee, one was a tax-collector, another a zealot.

The leader of the group is speaking. There is something arresting about his manner, and the words that fall from his lips are most interesting, " 'I have earnestly desired to eat this Passover with you before I suffer; for I tell you I shall not eat it until it is fulfilled in the kingdom of God.' And he took a cup, and when he had given thanks he said, 'Take this, and divide it among yourselves; for I tell you that from now on I shall not drink of the fruit of the vine until the kingdom of God comes.' And he took bread, and when he had given thanks he broke it and gave it to them, saying, 'This is my body which is given for you; this do in remembrance of me.' Likewise also the cup after supper, saying, 'This cup is the new covenant in my blood which is shed for you' " (*Luke* 22:15-20).

As the 14th of *Nisan** drew to a close and Passover lambs were being offered, the Lamb of God shed his blood outside the city walls. He died on a Roman cross bearing the curse of sin for the whole of mankind.

The promise given five hundred years before to Jeremiah was fulfilled, and the New Covenant was ratified.

The Eternal God of Israel, blessed be He, is a covenant-keeping God. Built into the terms of the New Covenant is the promise of universal blessing when all shall know Him, from the least unto the greatest, and only then, by recognizing Jesus as the sacrificial Lamb, will the last part of the new covenant be fulfilled: "I will be their God, and they shall be My people . . . for I will forgive their iniquity, and their sin will I remember no more" (*Jeremiah* 31:33, 34).

# *Immortality in Jewish Thought*

By VICTOR BUKSBAZEN

"Dear Mr. Segal: Is there a heaven and if so, what are my chances of getting there?"

So wrote an elderly Jewish lady to the late columnist, Alfred Segal.

"Maybe you can tell us where, if any place, we are all going from here. My husband and I, since we are well along in years, from time to time ask ourselves that question, but we never get an answer. What is your idea and what does our TENACH* say about it?"

To this anguished inquiry Mr. Segal had no definite answer.

There are millions of people who, like that Jewish lady, are asking with mounting anxiety: "Where do we go from here?" "Is there a heaven?" "What must I do to obtain eternal life?"

Sooner or later all of us will have to face this important question: "Where do we go from here?"

Let us turn to the TENACH* and investigate the Jewish teachings on this subject through the centuries.

Upon rising in the morning every pious Jew is enjoined to say the following prayer:

"O my God, the soul which thou gavest me is pure; thou didst create it, thou didst form it, thou didst breathe it into me; thou preservest it within me; and thou wilt take it from me, but wilt restore it unto me hereafter. So long as the soul is within me, I will give thanks unto Thee, O Lord my God and God of my fathers, Sovereign of all works, Lord of all souls! Blessed art Thou, O Lord, who restorest souls unto dead bodies" (*Daily Prayers,* Stern, p. 14).

Such has been the faith of traditional Judaism throughout the ages in the immortality of the soul and in the resurrection of the body.

The TENACH* does not set out to prove that man is immortal. It assumes it, just as it assumes the existence of God, without attempting to prove it. God is the source of all reality, He is the supreme Reality. The soul is immortal because He who created the soul of man is Himself immortal.

The Book of Genesis tells that God is the Creator of all life, whether plant, animal, or human. Only of man has it been said that he was created in the image and likeness of God.

> AND GOD SAID: LET US MAKE MAN IN OUR IMAGE, AFTER OUR LIKENESS ... AND GOD CREATED MAN IN HIS OWN IMAGE, IN THE IMAGE OF GOD CREATED HE HIM; MALE AND FEMALE CREATED HE THEM (*Genesis* 1:26, 27).

The somber view expressed in Ecclesiastes does not represent the faith of Solomon but rather the position of perplexed man who looks at life apart from God.

> FOR THAT WHICH BEFALLETH THE SONS OF MEN BEFALLETH BEASTS; EVEN ONE THING BEFALLETH THEM; AS THE ONE DIETH, SO DIETH THE OTHER; YEA, THEY HAVE ALL ONE BREATH; SO THAT MAN HATH NO PREEMINENCE ABOVE A BEAST; FOR ALL IS VANITY. ALL GO UNTO ONE PLACE; ALL ARE OF THE DUST, AND ALL RETURN TO DUST (*Ecclesiastes* 3:19, 20)

Solomon's real faith in the immortality of man is reflected in the following passages:

> AND THE DUST RETURNETH TO THE EARTH AS IT WAS, AND THE SPIRIT RETURNETH UNTO GOD WHO GAVE IT (*Ecclesiastes* 12:7).

Perhaps the clearest statement of faith in the immortality of man has been voiced by Job:

> I KNOW THAT MY REDEEMER LIVETH, AND THAT HE WILL WITNESS AT THE LAST UPON THE DUST; AND WHEN AFTER MY SKIN THIS IS DESTROYED, THEN WITHOUT MY FLESH SHALL I SEE GOD; WHOM I, EVEN I, SHALL SEE FOR MYSELF, AND MINE EYES SHALL BEHOLD, AND NOT ANOTHER'S (*Job* 19:25-27).

Coming to the Psalms we find numerous passages which clearly express faith in eternal life, life with God beyond the grave:

> I SHALL BEHOLD THY FACE IN RIGHTEOUSNESS; I SHALL BE SATISFIED, WHEN I AWAKE, WITH THY LIKENESS (*Psalm* 17:15).

> GOD WILL REDEEM MY SOUL FROM THE POWER OF THE NETHER WORLD; FOR HE SHALL RECEIVE ME (*Psalm* 49:16).

The same faith in the final victory of God over death is also expressed by the Prophet Isaiah:

> HE WILL SWALLOW UP DEATH FOREVER (*Isaiah* 25:8).

It is interesting to note that a similar faith in God's final victory over death is expressed in the well-known Passover song, "Had Gadya"—Only one Kid, which closes with the following passage:

> "THEN CAME THE MOST HOLY, BLESSED BE HE, AND SLEW THE ANGEL OF DEATH . . ."

Here we have an echo of Saul-Paul's words:

> THE LAST ENEMY TO BE DESTROYED IS DEATH (*I Corinthians* 15:26).

The vision of the valley of dry bones in *Ezekiel* 37:1-28, while it applies primarily to the resurrection of Israel as a nation, nevertheless presupposes the faith in the resurrection of the individual person without which national resurrection would be inconceivable. The dramatic description of the physical resurrection is here used as a figure of national resurrection:

> SO I PROPHESIED AS I WAS COMMANDED; AND AS I PROPHESIED, THERE WAS A NOISE, AND BEHOLD A COMMOTION, AND THE BONES CAME TOGETHER, BONE TO ITS BONE. AND I BEHELD, AND, LO, THERE WERE SINEWS UPON THEM, AND FLESH CAME UP, AND SKIN COVERED THEM ABOVE; BUT THERE WAS NO BREATH IN THEM.
>
> THEN SAID HE UNTO ME: "PROPHESY UNTO THE BREATH, PROPHESY, SON OF MAN, AND SAY TO THE BREATH: THUS SAITH THE LORD GOD: COME FROM THE FOUR WINDS, O BREATH, AND BREATHE UPON THESE SLAIN, THAT THEY MAY LIVE." SO I PROPHESIED AS HE COMMANDED ME, AND THE BREATH CAME INTO THEM, AND THEY LIVED, AND STOOD UP UPON THEIR FEET, AN EXCEEDING GREAT HOST (*Ezekiel* 37:7-10).

In this majestic scene the resurrection is visualized as a recreation of the bodies of men by the power of God's command and God's breath.

Again in *Daniel* 12:2:

> AND MANY OF THEM THAT SLEEP IN THE DUST OF THE EARTH SHALL AWAKE, SOME TO EVERLASTING LIFE, AND SOME TO REPROACHES AND EVERLASTING ABHORRENCE.

When we come to literature covering the 400 year period between the TENACH* and the New Testament, we have an ever growing volume of testimony to the faith of the Jews in the immortality of the soul and the resurrection of the body.

The literature of this period is known as the Apocrypha and the Pseudepigrapha.

Apocrypha is a Greek word which means the hidden or mystical writings. Later it took on the connotation of legendary or spurious literature. These writings, though considered as helpful and edifying, were not included in the canon of the Bible, and were never considered as God-inspired.

Nevertheless, the Apocrypha and Pseudepigrapha are important as historical documents from which we are able to learn about the beliefs of Jews in the period between the TENACH* and the New Testament.

Of special importance to our subject is *The Book of Enoch,* approximately middle second century B.C.E. There the fate of the righteous in the hereafter is thus described:

"And the righteous and elect shall be saved on that day,

And they shall never thenceforward see the face of the sinners and unrighteous.

And the Lord of Spirits will abide over them (*Enoch* 62:13-15).

On the other hand the fate of the unrighteous is pictured in this manner:

"Now they will say unto themselves: 'Our souls are full of unrighteous gain, but it does not prevent us from descending from the midst thereof into the burden of Sheol.'

And after that their faces shall be filled with darkness

And shame before that Son of Man,

And they shall be driven from his presence,

And the sword shall abide before his face in their midst" (*Enoch* 63:10, 11).

According to the Book of Enoch, after death there will be judgment when God and the Messiah will be the Judge. Then will God and the Messiah be vindicated and triumph.

"In those days the Lord bade (them) to summon and testify to the children of earth concerning their wisdom: Show (it) unto them; for ye are their guides, and a recompense over the whole earth. For I and My Son will be united with them forever in the paths of uprightness in their lives; and ye shall have peace: rejoice, ye children of uprightness. Amen" (*Enoch* 105:1, 2).

The Apocalypse of *Baruch,* believed to have been written about the year 100 C. E., gives expression to the life of the hereafter in chapter 49:2; 51:10.

We note then that in the literature of the inter-testamental period faith in the immortality of the soul and the resurrection of the body became more emphatic and outspoken than in past centuries. This faith often has a strong resemblance to the New Testament teaching on the same subject.

When we come to that great collection of rabbinic literature known as the Talmud* (approximately 200 to 600 C. E.), we find there a vast storehouse of views and beliefs concerning immortality.

In the Mishnah,* the earliest part of the Talmud,* is the important treatise, Pirke Aboth, "The Sayings of the Fathers." There the following thoughts are expressed about the resurrection and future judgment:

"Rabbi Elazar ha-Kappar said: Envy, lust and vainglory shorten a man's life.

"He used to say: Those who are born are destined to die; those who are dead are destined to be brought to life again; and the living are destined to be judged. (It is for you) to know, proclaim and be sure that he is God. He is the Maker, he the Creator, he the Discerner, he the Judge, he the Witness, he the Complainant; it is he who will judge. Blessed be he in whose presence there is no wrongdoing, nor forgetting, nor partiality, nor taking of bribes" (*Pirke Aboth* 4:28, 29, Second Century C. E.).

The above passage may be considered the classic position of traditional Judaism in the matter of resurrection since the beginning of the Christian era.

The New Testament is the most reliable source of information concerning the views and divergent opinions among the Jews about immortality in the first century C. E. It must be remembered that the New Testament preceded by many generations the Talmud.* It is from the New Testament that we first learn that the Sadducees did not believe in the resurrection:

> AND SADDUCEES CAME TO HIM, WHO SAY THAT THERE IS NO RESURRECTION (*Mark* 12:18).
>
> FOR THE SADDUCEES SAY THAT THERE IS NO RESURRECTION, NOR ANGEL, NOR SPIRIT; BUT THE PHARISEES ACKNOWLEDGE THEM ALL (*Acts* 23:8).

The above passages also indicate that the Pharisees and the Rabbis shared the same faith in the resurrection with Jesus and the apostles.

It is clear that in biblical times, and for many centuries later, the Jews believed both in the immortality of the soul and the resurrection of the body. The ancient Jewish Prayer Book contains many expressions of this faith.

The 13th article of faith by the famous Maimonides, included in the Hebrew Prayer Book, reads as follows:

"I believe with perfect faith that there will be a resurrection of the dead at the time when it shall please the Creator, blessed be his name, and exalted be the remembrance of him forever and ever" (*Daily Prayers,* Stern, p. 88).

Only in modern times has there been a departure from the ancient faith of Israel. Reform Judaism, while not repudiating immortality of the soul, is vague on this subject. Privately, many liberal rabbis voice unbelief in immortality and resurrection. A Jewish funeral is generally a very sad affair, with much grieving and despair. Faith in the resurrection of the dead, so characteristic of the Christian, is woefully lacking.

In principle, Jews and Christians are agreed upon the resurrection of the body and life everlasting. Yet, as in so many other respects, the New Testament gives us a more complete and a more definite doctrine of the resurrection and immortality than can be found in any other Jewish writings.

> I AM THE RESURRECTION AND THE LIFE; HE WHO BELIEVES IN ME, THOUGH HE DIE, YET SHALL HE LIVE (*John* 11:25).

Saul-Paul teaches that the denial of the resurrection of the body leads to the denial of the resurrection of Jesus.

> NOW IF MESSIAH IS PREACHED AS RAISED FROM THE DEAD, HOW CAN SOME OF YOU SAY THAT THERE IS NO RESURRECTION OF THE DEAD? BUT IF THERE

IS NO RESURRECTION OF THE DEAD, THEN MESSIAH HAS NOT BEEN RAISED: IF MESSIAH HAS NOT BEEN RAISED, THEN OUR PREACHING IS IN VAIN AND YOUR FAITH IS IN VAIN . . . (*I Corinthians* 15:12-14).

What kind of body will the risen body be? Saul-Paul tells us that it will be a transformed body. Although it will have some element of identity with the old body, yet the resurrected body will be different, even as the new grain of wheat differs from the seed from which it sprung.

SO IT IS WITH THE RESURRECTION OF THE DEAD. WHAT IS SOWN IS PERISHABLE, WHAT IS RAISED IS IMPERISHABLE. IT IS SOWN IN DISHONOP, IT IS RAISED IN GLORY. IT IS SOWN IN WEAKNESS, IT IS RAISED IN POWER. IT IS SOWN A PHYSICAL BODY, IT IS RAISED A SPIRITUAL BODY. IF THERE IS A PHYSICAL BODY, THERE IS ALSO A SPIRITUAL BODY (*I Corinthians* 15:42-44).

Although the New Testament teaches the resurrection of all people, yet not every one may look forward with joy to the resurrection. Jesus warned his people with these words:

DO NOT MARVEL AT THIS; FOR THE HOUR IS COMING WHEN ALL WHO ARE IN THE TOMBS WILL HEAR HIS VOICE AND COME FORTH, THOSE WHO HAVE DONE GOOD, TO THE RESURRECTION OF LIFE, AND THOSE WHO HAVE DONE EVIL, TO THE RESURRECTION OF JUDGMENT (*John* 5:28, 29).

It is only those who have received Jesus as Messiah Saviour from sin and as Lord of their lives who have cause to look forward with joyful anticipation to the resurrection from the dead. These can, with Saul-Paul, exclaim in triumph:

"Death is swallowed up in victory.
O death, where is thy victory?
O death, where is thy sting?

The sting of death is sin, and the power of sin is the law. But thanks be to God who gives us the victory through our Lord Jesus the Messiah " (*I Corinthians* 15:54-57).

# Doubly Blest

By SHELDON SCHER

Moses approached us from the heights. My fathers and I looked to him for direction as prescribed by Him on highest.

And Moses showed us tablets and told us words and said: "Behold, I set before you this day a blessing and a curse: the blessing, if you shall hearken to the commandments of the Lord your God which I command you this day; and the curse, if you shall not hearken to the commandments of the Lord your God, but turn aside out of the way which I command you this day, to go after other gods, which you have not known" (*Deuteronomy* 11:26-28).

We remembered that the Lord our God has chosen us to do His bidding; to live the life to which no others are so called. We are His people and His blessings are upon us unless we choose to disregard him—in which case we are cursed. Cursed only because the Lord our God is granting to His people the desired effect as indicated by our actions and inactions.

I was among the first who shouted, "I want the Law! I'll keep the Law! I will be blest!"

And from the mouth of Moses softly and assuredly came the words, "As you will, my son, as you will."

Then, as adversities in life appeared and became greater and greater stumbling blocks, I thought, "I cannot have been chosen! And if I were chosen, who asked for it? I do not choose to be chosen. Someone up there must have made a mistake about me." I doubted and turned away from His Word.

But our God makes no mistakes. I am His creation and have erred, but He is divine, He forgives. He forgave me and showed it when He did as His prophets said He would: He was born a man to teach His love and His way; to shed His light for me and all His people, for we were chosen above all.

He loves me so greatly that He made of Himself a holy sacrifice, that if I chose to accept Him, His blood might wash my slate clean.

But I chose to refute Him, just as I had ignored His choosing earlier.

I again disclaimed my birthright and said, "No! I will do for myself; I will decide; I will judge as I have in the past."

Then again as adversities in life became greater and greater stumbling blocks to happiness and seemed to overpower my will, I endeavored to reclaim my birthright and prayed, "God, if I am truly of the chosen people, what have I done to deserve this?"

And I heard, or felt, or knew, "It is not what you have done but what you have not done."

And so I racked my brain: "I pay my taxes; the financial debts I have incurred are being met; I get along well with most people; I am kind to animals; I think about those less fortunate than I am and help them as best I can; I try to be a good husband; my kids don't go hungry, nor are their clothes threadbare; I don't drink or gamble; I don't use foul language too often."

Then I started searching in other areas, and was about at my wit's end when something unforgettable happened: my daughter was going to be married to a believer in the false god of the gentiles. What's more, she asked me not only to attend the ceremony but to accompany her down the aisle of a house of heathen worship.

No! I would not! No! We are Jews, and this should not be.

And then her love softened me. Not only was I not able, but I did not want to refuse my blessing to my daughter.

And the realization came upon me: "My daughter showed me love. She asked nothing from me. She was of age; she requested no financial assistance; she did not ask me to make a home for her and her husband-to-be in my house. All she wanted was for me to love her and give her my blessing.

My heart spoke again, "It is what you have not done." I had not loved my heavenly Father, and I had not tried to know His love.

I thought, "If I plead my love to Him, would He refuse to accompany me on this distasteful venture?"

The reply came as an unquestionable and loving directive, answering both my question and my daughter's plea: "Of course, I will accompany you wherever you go."

I was led back to the Word of God as revered by my father and his fathers before him. Within that holy Book is contained the basis of the prayers and writings which had been my only link with my God.

I studied the words and sayings of Moses and the Psalmists and the Prophets. I reread what my eyes had seen before but which my heart had not known. I was learning to seek.

The message was still the same, but my heart had changed. Now I heard the message for the first time. I recognized my hunger and thirst, and my starved and parched spirit was satisfied. There in God's Word were the answers for all the world to know.

The Messiah was to be raised up from among us to be a prophet like unto Moses (*Deuteronomy* 18:15, 18); he would be born of a virgin (*Isaiah* 7:14); in Bethlehem (*Micah* 5:1); would enter Jerusalem in triumph (*Zechariah* 9:9); would be rejected by his own people (*Psalm* 118:22) and betrayed by one of his followers (*Psalm* 41:10); he would be silent before his accusers (*Isaiah* 53:7), and as a result smitten and spat upon by those who declared him an enemy (*Isaiah* 50:6); mocked and taunted (*Psalm* 22:7-8); was to suffer with transgressors and pray for those who declared him an enemy (*Isaiah* 53:12); lots would be cast for his garment (*Psalm* 22:19), and he would be given vinegar and gall (*Psalm* 69:22); his bones would not be broken (*Numbers* 9:12); he was to be raised from the dead (*Psalm* 16:10), and take his place at the right hand of God (*Psalm* 110:1).

These qualifications fit One who is described in my father's Scriptures: He is the Son of God, the promised Messiah.

And what of this Messiah? Is he unreachable in the distant heavens?

No, he is not hard to find. He is the living Son of the living Father, and his life and words and teachings are found in the continuation of the Holy Scriptures, the New Testament.

I studied and read. Then suddenly, though I had erred, I knew I had forgiveness; though I had been cursed, I knew I have been blest; though I had not loved God, I knew He loved me.

And so the blessing is mine, and I am able to satisfy my obligations and responsibilities as a Jew through Jesus the Messiah, the Saviour of Israel.

I became a free lance seeker of more knowledge, and gained more spiritually than I ever dreamed possible. Now I am no longer indifferent to my responsibilities as a Jew. I have found my vineyard, and as a Messianic Jew am now blest as a Jew by birthright, and doubly blest as a completed and confirmed believer in the promised Messiah.

# QUESTION BOX

**Question:** *Does not the New Testament give a wrong picture of the Pharisees? How then can it be reliable?*

**Answer:** The reference in *Matthew* 23:13 ff., is indeed harsh, but the New Testament does not regard all Pharisees as hypocrites as can be seen in *John* 3:1; *Luke* 7:36; 14:1. In fact, Saul-Paul was himself "a Pharisee, a son of Pharisees" (*Acts* 23:6).

There is a sense in which Jesus is much milder in his characterization of the Pharisees than are the Rabbis. Both the Jerusalem and the Babylonian TALMUDS* speak of seven types of Pharisees, six of whom are motivated insincerely and only one being "a Pharisee from love (of God)" *Sota* 22*b*.

Nowhere in the New Testament will you find an expression as "the plague of Pharisees" but you will find it in the TALMUD.* In the opinion of many TANAIM,* "a foolish pietist, a cunning rogue, a female Pharisee, and the plague of Pharisees bring destruction upon the world" (*Mishnah Sota* p. 102).

The Jerusalem TALMUD* relates that when one of the disciples of R. Yehudah Ha-Nasi had been victimized by some sharper, the Rabbi sorrowfully replied: "as for this man, he is afflicted by the plague of Pharisees" (*Sota* 3, 4).

It would be altogether incomprehensible had Jesus not called attention to the insincerity and hypocrisy of the Pharisees and had he not condemned them.

**Question:** *In discussing with our Rabbi* Genesis *49:10, "The sceptre shall not depart from Judah, nor the ruler's staff from between his feet, as long as men come to Shiloh; and unto him shall the obedience of the people be," he insists that there is no Messianic implication in this passage, and that Jews at no time applied it thus.*

**Answer:** It is somewhat surprising that the Rabbi is unfamiliar with the rabbinic interpretation of this prophecy. In *Midrash Rabbah* we read, "Until Shiloh come; this is the King Messiah" (*Gen. Rabb.* 98:13).

Also: "And to him is the gathering of the peoples; it is he to whom the nations of the world will gather, according to the text, 'The root of Jesse, that standeth for an ensign of the peoples, unto him shall the nations seek' (*Isaiah* 11:10)" *Gen. Rabb.* 99:10.

This prophecy in Genesis does point to the Messiah Jesus; the nations certainly have gathered to him, and Judah today is without lawgiver or king. The prophecy has therefore long since been fulfilled.

**Question:** *In Saul-Paul's letter to the* Romans, *chapter 11:26, are these words, "And so all Israel will be saved; as it is written, The Deliverer will come from Zion, he will banish ungodliness from Jacob." The original quotation in* Isaiah *59:20, however, reads, "And a redeemer will come to Zion, and unto them that turn from transgression in Jacob."*

**Answer:** The words of Saul-Paul correspond very closely to the Septuagint,* or Greek version of the TENACH.* Scholars are of the opinion that our Hebrew text in this instance is not above suspicion.

Many hold that where the Masoretic text has "unto them that turn from transgression in Jacob," the older text has preserved in the Septuagint,* "He shall turn away ungodliness from Jacob."

The Targum* has "to bring back the rebelliousness of the House of Jacob to the Law." The Hebrew, the Septuagint,* Saul-Paul, and the Targum* agree in the general sense of the passage, which is, that the coming of the Messiah shall be contemporary with the removal of sin in Jacob.

In this hope Christians and Jews are one.

**Question:** *I fail to see any perceptible difference between the Golden Rule of Hillel and that of Jesus. If there is a difference, kindly point it out.*

**Answer:** The Golden Rule of Jesus runs, "Whatever you wish that men would do to you, do so to them" (*Matthew* 7:12; *Luke* 6:31), and that of Hillel, "What is hateful to you, do not to your neighbour" (*Shabbath* 31*a*, p. 140).

Hillel's dictum has a counterpart in the Apocrypha, in the book of *Tobit* 4:15, where we read, "Do that to no man which thou hatest." The Chinese, too, have a precept ascribed to Confucius, "What you do not want done to yourself, do not to others."

The Hillel, the Tobit, and the Chinese precepts express the negative side of the Golden Rule, while that of Jesus is positive. There is a world of difference between the two concepts. "Do not" states the negative side and is good as far as it goes. The man who obeys Hillel or Confucius will do no harm, and that is something. The harmless man stands on a higher plane than the man who injures others. But "do" is the positive form of the rule, and the man who does good is vastly superior to the merely harmless man.

One can stand on the bank of a stream and watch another drown without lifting a hand to aid and yet not violate the "do not" of Hillel or Confucius, but he will violate the "do" of the Messiah Jesus.

**Question:** *Will you explain why* Matthew *gives forty-two generations from Abraham to Jesus, while according to* Luke *there were fifty-six?*

**Answer:** In the TENACH* (the Ketuvin*) *Ezra* (chapter 7:1-5) omits six important names from Amariah to Johanan. Matthew, being a Jew, merely utilized a method familiar to every rabbinical student.

Matthew's statement in chapter 1, verse 17: "So all the generations from Abraham to David were fourteen generations, and from David to the deportation to Babylon fourteen generations, and from the deportation to Babylon to the Messiah fourteen generations."

Matthew's genealogy is a summary of Jewish history. In this list are three groups of fourteen names each and was evidently suggested by the name of David which in Hebrew has the numerical value of fourteen: daled = 4, vov = 6, daled = 4. This is in keeping with the rabbinic method of mnemonics, or aid to memory.

The learned Dr. Solomon Schechter, for many years president of the Jewish Theological Seminary of America, remarking on the thoroughly rabbinic character of Matthew's genealogy wrote, "The impression conveyed to the rabbinic student by the perusal of the New Testament is, in many parts, like that gained by reading an old rabbinic homily."

In Jewish writings, mere exactness in numerals easily gives way to mnemonics and hortatory instruction. No really learned Jew would dream of making an issue of the genealogy of the first Gospel on this score.

**Question:** *How do you explain the account that Jesus was the Son of God, of the house of David? Either Jesus was the natural offspring of Joseph and Mary and therefore not the Son of God; or he was conceived by the Holy Spirit, Joseph not being his father, and was therefore not a descendant of the house of David because Mary was not of that house."*

**Answer:** It is obvious that the difficulty here is because of an "either-or" attitude. Why assume that Jesus could not have been the Son of God if he had been born in the ordinary way as the natural offspring of Joseph and Mary?

The incarnation, or God becoming man, is an extraordinary act of God, and would have been no less so had it taken place in the ordinary way.

Granted that the birth of Jesus was miraculous, what about the birth of Isaac? or Samuel? or the Baal Shem Tov?

Furthermore, why assume that Mary was not a descendant of the house of David? The Bible doesn't say that she wasn't. According to the Talmud,* "The family of the father is regarded (as the proper) family (but) the family of the mother is not regarded (as the proper) family" (*Baba Bathra,* 109*b*, p. 452).

Archaeologists have found tablets which throw light on the custom of having people report to their ancestral cities for the purpose of "enrollment," or census, or taxation. If a husband and wife were from different "houses" each would report to his own place. In the second chapter of *Luke* we read that "Joseph went up from Galilee, from the city of Nazareth, to Judea, to the city of David, which is called Bethlehem, because he was of the house and lineage of David, to be enrolled with Mary, his betrothed, who was with child" (vs. 4-5).

The best proof that Jesus was the Son of David is the record that says so plainly; that the circumstances of his birth were known to everyone; that throughout his ministry he was addressed as the Son of David; and no one ever questioned it.

This would certainly create the strongest kind of assumption that both Joseph, his legal father, and Mary, his natural mother, were descendants of the house of David.

„זיי מוחל, פּאָטער מיינער, זיי מוחל. איך האָב עובֿר געווען קעגן דיר, אַ גרויסער גאָט. כ'ווייס אַז גרויס איך מיין חטא, און תּאַוואַהדיק שלעכט זענען מיינע מעשׂים.

„טאַטע, פּאָטער, דיין ליבשאַפט קער מיר אום! כּוח גיב מיר, אָ, רוח־הקודש! לעבן וויל איך מיט עמנואלן. אַ לויב און אַ דאַנק ישועו, מיין גואל."

נאָך דעם דאָזיקן צוזאַמענקונפט האָבן איך זיך נאָך באַגעגנט, אין משך פון שבתדיקן טאָג מיט אַ סך קונקער ייִדן.

## דאָס לעבן ציט זיך ווייטער

שבת צו נאַכט האָב איך נאָך באַזוכט זייער פאָרשטייער, כוּאַן דע דיִאָס לאַ טאָררע, כּדי זיך צו געזעגענען מיט אים. ביי אים אין שטוב האָט מען באמת געקענט מאַכן די ברכה פון „המבדיל בין קודש לחול".

אין דער שטוב, וואו סע האָט אַ גאַנצן טאָג געשוועבט הייליקע רו און מנוחה, האָט די נאַכט מיט זיך אַריינגעבראַכט דעם וואָכנדיקן אומרו אין די טרחה.

איך האָב מיך וואַרעם און פריינטלעך געזעגנט מיט דער פאַמיליע לאַ טאָררע, מיט זייערע אָנגעשטעלטע און האָב געמיינט, אַז איך וועל שוין מער ניט זען, פאַר מיין אָפּרייזע, קיין קונקער ייִדן.

ערשט גאַנץ פרי, אַזייגער 7 איז צו מיר געקומען זיך געזעגענען, אין דער באַגלייטונג פון איר פלימעניצע ראַקל, מאַריאַ דע לאַ כּאַראַ.

מיט דער דאָזיקער אינטערעסאַנטער פאָרשטייערן פון די קונקער ייִדן, האָב איך געכאַפּט דעם לעצטן שמועס.

זי האָט מיט אַזויפיל האַרץ, מיט אַזויפיל וואַרעמקייט גערעדט וועגן די ליידן פון ייִדישן פאָלק; האָט מיט אַזויפיל האָפענונגען און גלויבן גערעדט וועגן דער גאולה, פון דעם ייִדישן פאָלק, און דערביי זענען אירע גרויסע, ברוינע אויגן באַפינקלט געוואָרן מיט אַ פּאָר ריינע, בריליאַנטענע טרערן, אַז עס האָט געקאָנט רירן דעם קאַלטסטן און אומגלייביקסטן.

זי האָט מיך אַרויסבאַגלייט צום באַן, ווי מען באַגלייט אַרויס עפּעס דעם ליבסטן און זעלטענסטן גאַסט.

אירע גרויסע אויגן, באַצירט מיט די פּאָר פינקלנדיקע טרערן, האָבן מיך ווייט, ווייט באַגלייט. זיי האָבן מיך אויך באַגלייט דאַן, ווען די באַן האָט זיך שוין גערירט. זיי האָבן מיך באַגלייט, ווען איך האָב זי שוין מער ניט געזען.

און געטראַכט האָב איך בעת־מעשׂה: אויב דער כּוס פון ייִדישע טרערן איז נאָך אַלץ ניט פאַרפולט, דאַרף ער איבערגעפולט ווערן מיט מאַריאַ דע לאַ כּאַראַס הייליקע, כּשרע טרערן...

ווער זענען זיי, אָט די דאָזיקע קונקער ייִדן? וויאַזוי קומען זיי אייגנטלעך קיין קונקאָ? וועלכע זענען זייערע מִנהָגים, און אין וואָס באַשטייט זייער ייִדישקייט? אויף די און אַנדערע פֿראַגעס וועל איך דאָ טאַקע זוכן צו געבן אַן ענטפֿער.

אָנגעקומען קיין קונקאָ, בין איך, ווי אַ פֿרומער, ערלעכער ייִד עֶרֶב־שַׁבָּת פֿאַר שקִיעת־הַחַמה. איך האָב געוואָלט זען ווי די קונקער זענען מקַבּל שַׁבּת.

נאָכגעפֿרעגט אויף זיי האָבן איך זיך בײַ דעם ערשטן 12־יאָריקן ייִנגל, וואָס איך האָב אויף דער גאַס געטראָפֿן. צי ווייסט ער ניט – האָב איך אים געפֿרעגט – וואו סע געפֿינט זיך די שול פֿון די, וואָס היטן אָפּ שַׁבּת. דאָס ייִנגל האָט מיר אָנגעוויזן אויף אַ זײַטיק געסל. איך האָב מיך אַהין געלאָזן.

## צו קבלת־שבת

בײַ דער טיר פֿון דער שול בין איך אומאַנטשלאָסן שטיין געבליבן: אַרײַנגיין? קווײַנקלענדיק זיך אַזוי, האָב איך מיך דערווײַל צוגעהערט צו דעם געזאַנג, וואָס האָט זיך אַרויסגעטראָגן פֿון דער שול און זיך איבערגעגאָסן אין דער געדיכטער פֿינצטערניש פֿון די קונקער געסלעך.

פּלוצלונג האָט זיך דאָס געזאַנג אָפּגעשטעלט און איך האָב באַשלאָסן דאָך אַרײַנצוגיין. צום באַדויערן האָב איך זיך מיט די מִתפּללִים אָנגעטראָפֿן בײַם שוועל פֿון דער שול. די עטלעכע מִניָנים מִתפּללִים האָבן אויסגעזען ניט ווי קיין פֿרעמדע צווישן זיך, נאָר ווי אַ גרויסע מִשפּחה. זיי האָבן זיך צוליב מײַן כָּבוד ווענן צוריק אומגעקערט אין שול אַרײַן, כּדי צו כאַפּן מיט מיר אַ שמועס.

זיי האָבן בײַ מיר זיך אַלץ געוואָלט דערוויסן וואָס מערער און מערער ייִדישע דִינים און מִנהָגים, און איך האָב דערווײַל געזען זייער בקִיאות.

אויף מײַן פֿראַגע, צו זיי נוצן וועלכע ניט איז סִידורים, האָבן זיי געענטפֿערט, אַז זיי בעטן דאָס, וואָס זיי קומט אויף דער מַחשָבה.

אין מײַנע פֿראַגעס בין איך אָפּטמאָל געווען אַביסל צודרינגלעך און דירעקט. אַזוי, לְמָשל, האָב איך גאַנץ ייִדישלעך אַרויסגענומען – זאָגנדיק דערבײַ ווי עס פּירט זיך „קאָן סו פּערמִיסאָ" – מיט אייער דערלויבעניש – פֿון די הענט פֿון זייערן אַ נִכבד, דעם בוך, וואָס ער האָט געהאַלטן.

דאָס איז געווען אַ תּנַ"ך מיטן בּרית חַדָשָה צוזאַמען געבונדן, אין שפּאַניש. בלעטערנדיק אים האָב איך דאָרטן געפֿונען אַ פּאַפּירל, אויף וועלכן עס איז געווען אָפּגעדרוקט אַ תּפִילה, וואָס איז שטאַרק פּאָפּולער בײַ זיי. די תּפִילה הייסט „פּאַרדאָן פּאַטרע מִיאַ, סִי פּאַרדאָן" – זיי מוחל פֿאָטער מײַנער.

דאָ וועל איך די לעזער באַקענען מיט דער אויבנדערמאָנטער תּפִילה אין מײַן ייִדישער איבערזעצונג:

# אַ גאַסט אויף שבת

## פון חיים ראַפּאָפּאָרט

טיף אין ווייטן דָרום, פון דעם ווייטן, ווייטן זיד־אַמעריקע, אין דער מדינה טשילע, ביי אַ 450 מייל פון דער הויפּט־שטאָט סאַנטיאַגאָ, ליגט דאָס שטעטעלע פּרייֵרע.

רחָבותדיק ברייט זענען די גאַסן פון פּרייֵרע און ענִיוֹותדיק קליין שטייען איבער זיי די הייזלעך צעשטעלט. ליגט די זון אַ גאַנצן טאָג צעלייגט איבער דער גאַנצער ברייט פון דער פּרייֵרער גאַס. ניטאָ קיין ברעקל שאָטן, וואָס זאָל זי פאַרשטעלן. בראָט זי און סמאַליעט ווי אַ קאַלך־אויוון. זעט מען קיין לעבעדיקן מענטשן ניט אָן פאַר די אויגן אויף די גאַסן פון פּרייֵרע.

נאָר יעדן פאַרנאַכט, ווען די זון הייבט זיך אָן צו פאַררוקן אונטער די בערג, ווערט איר רו געשטערט...

סאָפּנדיק און פּעכנדיק, מיט רַעש און רוגזה, מיט דער רוגזה פון אַן אֱמֶתן גַזלן, לויפט אַלע פאַרנאַכט אָן אַהער די שטאָלענע חַיה – די באַן.

זי שטעלט זיך אָפּ אויף אַ ווײַלע, וואַרפט אַרויס פון איר לאַנגען עק עטלעכע פאַרשוין מיט זייערע זעקלעך און פּעקלעך, כאַפּט אויף שנעל אַ שלוק וואַסער, אָטעמט שטאַרק אָפּ און לויפט ווייטער.

אונדזער באַן הויבט אָן דורכצורייסן די געדיכטע רויך־וואָלקנס, און פאַר די אויגן אונדזערע טיילט זיך אַרויס דאָס שטעטעלע קונקאָ.

## אַ נייער יידישער שבט

אָט דאָס דאָזיקע, צוויי־זילביקע, אינדיש וואָרט, „קונקאָ", איז דאָס דער ערשטער פּאָדים, פון וועלכן עס האָט זיך דאָ פאַרוועבט די לעגענדע פון אַ ניי־אַנטדעקטן יידישן שֵבֶט אין טשילע.

ווער האָט עס אַנטדעקט אָט דעם נייעם יידישן שֵבֶט, וואָס געפינט זיך אין די טיפע, אוראַלטע וועלדער, אין דעם ווייטן דָרום פון לאַנד?

די, וואָס קענען די געשיכטע פון טשילענער יונגען יידישן ישוב, ווייסן, אַז מיט אַן עֶרֶך 17–18 יאָר צוריק, האָט זיך אַ טשילענער דערלעגאַציע פון דָרום־געגנט געווענדט צו דעם דעמאָלסדיקן ציוניסטישן לאַנד־קאָנגרעס מען זאָל אים אויפנעמען.

און ווי דערשטוינט דער דעמאָלסדיקער קאָנגרעס איז געוואָרן, דערהערנדיק פון די טשילענער, אַז זיי זענען יידן, און דערצו נאָך ציוניסטן.

# *By Faith*

By MOISHE ROSEN

BY FAITH ABRAHAM, WHEN HE WAS TESTED, OFFERED UP ISAAC, AND HE WHO HAD RECEIVED THE PROMISES WAS READY TO OFFER UP HIS ONLY SON, OF WHOM IT WAS SAID, "THROUGH ISAAC SHALL YOUR DESCENDANTS BE NAMED." HE CONSIDERED THAT GOD WAS ABLE TO RAISE MEN EVEN FROM THE DEAD; HENCE, FIGURATIVELY SPEAKING, HE DID RECEIVE HIM BACK (*Hebrews* 11:17-19).

Even though rabbinical Judaism has modified God's original revelation, there are certain vestigial remains of a religion that is much closer in doctrine to Christianity than the modern teaching of the Rabbis. The following is from the *High Holyday Prayer Book,* p. 342:

> OUR GOD AND THE GOD OF OUR FATHERS, REMEMBER US FAVORABLY AND VISIT US WITH MERCIFUL DELIVERANCE FROM THE ETERNAL HIGH HEAVENS. REMEMBER IN OUR FAVOR, LORD OUR GOD, THE COVENANT, THE KINDNESS, AND THE SOLEMN PROMISE WHICH THOU DIDST MAKE TO OUR FATHER ABRAHAM ON MOUNT MORIAH; BE MINDFUL OF THE TIME WHEN OUR FATHER ABRAHAM BOUND HIS SON ISAAC ON THE ALTAR, SUPPRESSING HIS COMPASSION THAT HE MIGHT DO THY WILL

WHOLEHEARTEDLY. MAY THY MERCY LIKEWISE HOLD BACK THY ANGER FROM US; IN THY GREAT GOODNESS, MAY THY WRATH TURN AWAY FROM THY PEOPLE, THY CITY, THY LAND, THY HERITAGE. FULFILL, LORD OUR GOD, WHAT THOU HAST PROMISED US IN THY TORAH* THROUGH MOSES THY SERVANT: "IN THEIR FAVOR I WILL REMEMBER THE COVENANT MADE WITH THEIR ANCESTORS, WHOM I BROUGHT OUT OF THE LAND OF EGYPT IN SIGHT OF THE NATIONS, TO BE THEIR GOD; I AM THE LORD" (*Leviticus* 26:45).

THOU WHO DOST EVER REMEMBER ALL FORGOTTEN THINGS, FOR THERE IS NO FORGETTING BEFORE THY THRONE OF GLORY, MAYEST THOU ON THIS DAY MERCIFULLY REMEMBER THE BINDING OF ISAAC IN FAVOR OF HIS DESCENDANTS. BLESSED ART THOU, O LORD, WHO DOST REMEMBER THE COVENANT.

As part of the New Year Feast of Trumpets observance, Orthodox Jews pray this strange prayer—that God would bring salvation and turn away Divine wrath at sin because Abraham offered his son, Isaac, as a sacrifice. Most Jews either don't know this prayer or skip over the spiritual significance.

On the Feast of Trumpets, which has come to be regarded as the New Year—*Rosh Hashanah*—the service is initiated by the eerie sound of a ram's horn sounded by a holy man from the synagogue. The Rabbis explain this as a memorial—God sent a ram to be killed in the stead of Isaac. Isaac was saved by a substitute sacrifice. The ram's horn trumpet or shofar is important to herald men to repentance.

But lost in the conflicting and opposing ideas of Judaism is the prayer, "Hear us because Abraham was ready to offer up his only son!"

Contemporary Jewish leaders are quick to take exception with Christian doctrine. They point out that Christianity says all men are sinful and need an intercessor to have reconciliation with God and atonement, but Judaism teaches that there is no need for an intercessor and one can go directly to God. This is an oversimplification of what Christians believe, and a misrepresentation of the ancient Jewish religion.

Christians believe that there is not only the need of an intercessor, but there is also the necessity of having a basis of intercession. That basis for intercession is the shed blood of the Intercessor at Calvary which becomes the basis of reconciliation.

The many references to the *Akedah,* the binding of Isaac, as a basis for hearing prayer seem to prove that ancient Jews, like biblical Christians, found it necessary to have not only an intercessor, but grounds of intercession.

Furthermore, after the time of Abraham's offering up of Isaac, God instituted the Jewish religion with a system of intercessors (the priesthood), and a continuing basis of intercession through the sacrificial system. We therefore must maintain that Christianity, as revealed in the New Testament and practiced today, is more Jewish in its adherence to original revelation than is modern Rabbinic Judaism.

The ancient Rabbis misunderstood the meaning of the *Akedah.* They saw as the ground of intercession the fact that Abraham was a righteous man, completely obedient to God. Yet we know that Abraham was not absolutely righteous, nor was Moses nor King David. All of them were men who sinned and needed atonement themselves. The TENACH* speaks of the righteousness of Abraham where it says, "Abraham believed in the Lord; and He counted it to him for righteousness" (*Genesis* 15:6). Abraham was saved by faith, and even so, Jews, Gentiles, people of every race, can be saved in the same way today, by faith.

The binding of Isaac as Abraham's sacrifice was considered central in the ancient Jewish religion. The prayer books and commentaries have much to say about the *Akedah.* It becomes the ground of prayer. That is to say, God is asked to grant forgiveness and hear petitions because Abraham offered up his son.

In this, God was teaching ancient Israel that the offering of His Son was the basis of reconciliation between God and man, not Isaac, for God provided a substitute for him. The TENACH* records that the substitute was a ram, but as Isaac was a type, even that ram was a type of the Lamb of God, His own Son, who would be offered for sin to effect reconciliation.

However, it is not an act of faith to make decisions to believe what is contrary to that which God has revealed in the TENACH.* It is not faith to fashion in our minds a God who is agreeable to us and then worship Him. It is not of faith to set man's tradition above revelation.

Some think that Jews who believe in Jesus have departed from the ancestral faith. This is not true. We have departed from the modern notions of Rabbis who have de-emphasized sin and salvation. We have departed from an ethnic humanism, which is man-centered rather than God-centered. But we have returned to the ancient religion of Abraham, Jacob, Moses, and David.

Most Jewish people, as they go to synagogue on *Rosh Hashanah,* will have had little idea of what the shofar means, how it speaks of Isaac, the *Akedah,* and the basis of prayer. It is ironic that these ancient truths are better understood by Gentile Christians than by Jewish people.

We, too, petition God on the basis of the giving of a son, not the son of Abraham, for Isaac was but a man, sinful as are we. God gave His own Son, His only begotten Son. He didn't stay the agony of death from Jesus as He did from Isaac.

Today, those who are Christians come before God because of the atonement accomplished, not at Mount Moriah, but at Mount Calvary.

Today, Christians who are both Jews and non-Jews are waiting for a trumpet call, but not the call to assemble at the synagogue, but a call to assemble with Jesus our Messiah.

„מִשפּט ניט, כּדֵי איר זאָלט ניט געמִשפּט ווערן" – יֵשוּעַ הַמָשִיחַ.

# Did the Jews Kill Christ?

By HENRY EINSPRUCH

Did the Jews kill Christ? No, says the modern Jew. And even Orthodox Jews who, as a rule, seek to avoid the subject, will insist that the Jews did not do it—it was the Romans. How then came Jews to be charged with the crime? Any Rabbi will tell you that the Gospels are to blame, and particularly is this true of the Gospel of John.

But supposing the Gospel of John, and for that matter the other three Gospels, those of Matthew, Mark, and Luke, should disappear, would we then escape the onus under which we are resting? Hardly. And for the following reason:

Both the Jerusalem and the Babylonian Talmuds* admit that Jews brought about the fate of Jesus. The Talmud* knows nothing of Romans, but makes the death of Jesus wholly a Jewish act. This is plain from the *Mishnah Sanhedrin,* 43*a*; 67*a*; and from the *Jerusalem Recension* VII, 16 (fol. 25*c* and *d*). It is true that the Talmud* does not say that Jews crucified Jesus, but it does say that he was both stoned and hung by Jews.

Are we then seeking to whitewash the Romans? No! A thousand times no! But the lie which shifts the blame of the crime on the Gospel writers ought to be exposed, and this in the interest of truth.

There is a passage in the *Acts* (the fifth book in the New Testament), chapter 4, verses 27 and 28:

> FOR TRULY IN THIS CITY THERE WERE GATHERED TOGETHER AGAINST THY HOLY SERVANT JESUS, WHOM THOU DIDST ANOINT, BOTH HEROD AND PONTIUS PILATE, WITH THE GENTILES AND THE PEOPLES OF ISRAEL, TO DO WHATEVER THY HAND AND THY PLAN HAD PREDESTINED TO TAKE PLACE.

These are plain, straightforward words. Herod was a bloodthirsty Idumean; Pontius Pilate was a Roman who despised Jews and crucified them by the score; the Gentiles are mentioned next in the order of culpability; and Israel is referred to last. These words, it should be remembered, were spoken by Peter, one of the earliest followers of Jesus whom Jewish tradition vests with rabbinical sanctity, ascribing to him the authorship of a number of synagogal hymns, including the *Nishmath kol chay* (The soul of every living thing), the metrical prayer recited on the Sabbath (see Jellinek's *Beth Ha Midrash,* vols. V-VI, Vienna, 1873, and Eisenstein's *Ozar Midrashim,* N.Y., 1915, Vol. II, pp. 557-559).

Crucifixion was not a Jewish mode of capital punishment, it was Roman, although there is a passage in Josephus showing that the Jewish king, Alexander Jannaeus, had 800 rebel Pharisees crucified (*Antiquities* XIII, 14*b*). Nowhere in the Gospels is it said that Jews did the crucifying. More than that, the Gospel of John, which is supposed to be anti-Jewish, makes it clear that Jews could not have done the actual crucifying since they did not possess the power to carry out a death sentence (*John* 18:31).

Now then what were the causes that led up to the death of Jesus? For the facts we must turn to historic documents. There we are told that Jesus, by his bold preaching and acts, came into conflict with the Temple authorities. In *Matthew* 21:12-13 and *John* 2:13-16 the account is given to us in this graphic setting:

Jesus, a loyal, obedient Jew, conscious of his messianic mission, made his way to Jerusalem for the Passover. Going into the Temple he was shocked to see that it had been turned into a business mart. Indignation welled up in his heart upon seeing God's holy place so prostituted and defiled by human greed. Calling to mind the words of *Jeremiah* (7:11) who declared that God's Temple was to be "a house whereupon My name is called," he drove out the racketeers, the money changers, the cattle-hucksters, and all who had turned God's house into a den of robbers.

This brought Jesus into open conflict with the Boethusean-High Priests. Jesus was in their way. He was daily gaining in popularity with the Jewish masses, and so they determined to do away with him. But is it possible that a High Priest of God would sink to such a level? Yes, anything can be believed about the Annas-Caiphas combine (*John* 18:13-14). There is a curious street ballad about them preserved for us in the Talmud* which runs as follows:

> WOE IS ME BECAUSE OF THE HOUSE OF BOETHUS; WOE IS ME BECAUSE OF THEIR STAVES!
> WOE IS ME BECAUSE OF THE HOUSE OF HANIN, WOE IS ME BECAUSE OF THEIR WHISPERINGS!
> WOE IS ME BECAUSE OF THE HOUSE OF KATHROS, WOE IS ME BECAUSE OF THEIR PENS!
> WOE IS ME BECAUSE OF THE HOUSE OF ISHMAEL THE SON OF PHABI, WOE IS ME BECAUSE OF THEIR FISTS!
> FOR THEY ARE HIGH PRIESTS AND THEIR SONS ARE (TEMPLE) TREASURERS AND THEIR SONS-IN-LAW ARE TRUSTEES AND THEIR SERVANTS BEAT THE PEOPLE WITH STAVES (*Pesahim* 57*a*, p. 285).

Jesus had attacked the institution which had proven so lucrative a gold mine to the priestly hierarchy. To go to the hated Gentile, the Roman Pontius Pilate, and complain that Jesus was interfering with a Jewish religious institution would only have met with contempt, hence a case was trumped up that he was a rebel against the empire, against Caesar. False witnesses were hired who claimed that they had heard Jesus say that he was the Jewish King. Jesus did not deny that he was the Messiah, the King of Israel.

Furthermore, the High Priest had a mock court condemn Jesus on religious grounds, and when Pilate was unwilling to meddle in a purely Jewish squabble he was charged with being partial to one who had declared himself a king, and so inimical to the interests of Caesar. When Pilate finally asked whether they were willing that he crucify the Jewish King, the mob of Boethusean High Priests shouted:

WE HAVE NO KING BUT CAESAR! (*John* 19:15).

Pilate then, under compulsion of the Jewish authorities, sentenced Jesus to die on a Roman cross. This is history.

Now to return to the question: Did the Jews kill Christ? This depends on whether the Boethusean High Priests were the representatives of the Jews, and whether what they did on that fatal day can be laid to the charge of the entire Jewish people.

This is written mainly for those who shout the loudest that Jews as such did not crucify Jesus. May we therefore submit the following:

Are you ready and willing to disavow the action of the Boethusean High Priests, the Annas and Caiphas clique?

Are you ready to grant that in that fatal Passover week, nearly two thousand years ago, a flagrant violation and miscarriage of justice took place in Israel against Jesus?

If you are not, then you must bear on your conscience the onus of the injustice crowned by wrong. There are Jews like Adolph Danziger who courageously admitted that in the case of Jesus every rule of the Torah* was trampled under foot, and who insisted that reparation, vindication, and expiation be made that justice perish not from the earth.

* * *

In a larger sense the death of Jesus was not an accident; the greed of the mercenary priests and the vacillation of Pontius Pilate were merely incidental to it. The New Testament teaches that the death of Christ was a Divine act, that his death was sacrificial; and the intelligent follower of Jesus, be he Jew or Gentile, does not shift the blame on the shoulders of the Jews, but assumes equal responsibility for the tragedy that took place on Golgotha's hill. There is a Christian litany, or penitential piyyut* which runs:

"WHO WAS THE GUILTY? WHO BROUGHT THIS UPON THEE?
ALAS MY TREASON HATH UNDONE THEE, JESUS,
'TWAS I, LORD JESUS, I IT WAS DENIED THEE:
I CRUCIFIED THEE."

* * *

The cleavage of the centuries can be bridged. The misunderstandings and hates which have kept Jew and Gentile apart can be removed by a common acknowledgement that in the person of the High Priest our people were led into a fatal act, and through Pontius Pilate and the Roman soldiery the whole Gentile world became sharers in the immolation of the Messiah.

We are equally guilty, both of us—Jew and Gentile—and have need to smite our breast and cry for the forgiveness of God. He will not reject us.

"A broken and a contrite heart, O God, Thou wilt not despise" (*Psalm* 51:19).

# *Trinity is Jewish*

By RACHMIEL FRYDLAND

Most Jewish people seem to have made their peace with Jesus of Nazareth. Some consider him to be a great Jew, or even the greatest Jew who ever lived. Some of our Jewish leaders, as Dr. Heinrich Graetz and Dr. Joseph Klausner, compliment him on his teaching. Some admire his parables and purity, as Moses Montefiore; and some, as Sholem Asch, consider him to be the Messiah of the Gentiles.

Today we often meet Jewish people who acknowledge that Jesus is the Messiah for Jew and Gentile alike. What then holds such people back from accepting him as their personal Messiah-Saviour?

The hindrance some have expressed is the reluctance to accept the fact that Jesus is supernatural. Moreover, from childhood we have been inculcated with Maimonides' Thirteen Principles, the second of which is:

"I believe with perfect faith that the Creator, blessed be his name, is a Unity, and that there is no unity in any manner like unto his, and that he alone is our God, who was, is, and will be."

The word *Unity* is derived from the verb to *unite.* All of its synonyms, such as join, combine, link, amalgamate, associate, coalesce, connect, couple, carry the thought of combining or conjoining in some manner so as to form *one* from that which is *more than one.*

Hebrew has two words for the expression ONE. The first is *yachid* יָחִיד which means *absolute;* the second is *echod* אֶחָד which means *unity.*

In *Deuteronomy* 6:4 is recorded: "Sh'ma Yisrael Adonai Elohenu Adonai Echod"—Hear, O Israel: the Lord our God, the Lord is One.

שְׁמַע יִשְׂרָאֵל יְהוָה אֱלֹהֵינוּ יְהוָה ׀ אֶחָד׃

*Echod* is also the word that Moses uses in *Genesis* 2:24 when he writes: "Therefore shall a man leave his father and his mother, and shall cleave unto his wife, and they shall be *one* flesh."

We have been brought up to think that if we believe that God is One, then this idea excludes any idea of God's triunity, and any possibility that God in the latter time manifested Himself through Jesus the Messiah. This concept of God's triunity seemed to us to be a Gentile and pagan idea. NOT SO! Christians as well as Jews must believe in One God. There is no other. The God of Abraham, Isaac, and Jacob is the God of the Jewish people and of the Christians. The Hebrew Scriptures are authoritative for the Jew and for the Christian.

While it is universally admitted by both Jews and Christians that God is One and that there is no one beside Him, we are also compelled to acknowledge that the triunity of God is clearly taught in the Torah,* the Prophets, and in the Writings—that is, in the whole TENACH,* the Hebrew Scriptures of the Old Testament and the New Testament. This concept is well known not only in the TENACH,* but also in Talmudical and rabbinical writings.

THE TORAH: When God *Elohim* created the world He wanted to make absolutely clear to His creation that He is not some abstract mathematical unitarian principle with no analogy in all creation, as some of our philosophers tried to present Him under Aristotelian influence. Instead we read in the Torah* (*Genesis* 1:1):

> IN THE BEGINNING GOD *ELOHIM* CREATED THE HEAVENS AND THE EARTH ... AND THE SPIRIT OF GOD *RUACH ELOHIM* HOVERED OVER THE FACE OF THE WATERS.

Was it as speaking for Himself and His Spirit that we have these words:

> AND GOD *ELOHIM* SAID: LET US MAKE MAN IN OUR IMAGE, AFTER OUR LIKENESS; AND LET THEM HAVE DOMINION OVER THE FISH OF THE SEA, AND OVER THE FOWL OF THE AIR, AND OVER THE CATTLE, AND OVER ALL THE EARTH (*Genesis* 1:26).

God *Elohim* made man in His image, a being composed of a triunity—body, soul, and spirit, and to make this more clear God reveals Himself in His plural form of *Elohim* and says, "Let *us* make man . . ."

Even those of our Rabbis who do not accept the triunity of God realize that this verse is clear support for such teaching. Thus in *Midrash Rabbah* on *Genesis* we find the following comments on this verse:

"Rabbi Samuel bar Nahman in the name of Rabbi Jonathan said, that at the time when Moses wrote the Torah,* writing a portion of it daily, when he came to this verse which says, 'And *Elohim* said, let us make man in our image after our likeness,' Moses said, Master of the Universe why do you give herewith an excuse to the sectarians (who believe in the triunity of God), God answered Moses, You write and whoever wants to err let him err."

But surely God did not make Moses write the whole Scriptures in order to make people err, but rather to show them the right way and the right revelation, namely, that the One God is a triune God who calls Himself *Elohim* and who says, *Let us make man.*

THE PROPHETS (NEVIIM): There are many Scripture verses which show clearly that God manifested Himself also as the Word by which He created heaven and earth and by which He leads and directs creation. He also manifested Himself as the *Ruach Hakodesh,* the Holy Spirit, who inspired the prophets of God and who did mighty miracles through the great judges of Israel, Gideon, Samson and others. We want to point out one Scripture which compels us to admit the triunity of God. Isaiah the prophet speaks in the name of God and says:

> COME YE NEAR UNTO ME, HEAR YE THIS: FROM THE BEGINNING I HAVE NOT SPOKEN IN SECRET; FROM THE TIME THAT IT WAS, THERE AM I; AND NOW THE LORD GOD HATH SENT ME, AND HIS SPIRIT (*Isaiah* 48:16).

Here God calls the people to come to Him, but He is sent by the Lord God and His Spirit. Exactly the same teaching as we have found in the Torah* we find also in the teachings of the prophets. How else can it be? The same God who commanded Moses to manifest His triunitarian nature commands also the Hebrew prophets to do the same.

THE WRITINGS (KETHUBIN): Very clearly we find the same teaching about God in the Psalms and in the other writings of the Hebrew Scriptures. We read in *Psalm* 2, verse 2, where the Holy Spirit, the *Ruach Hakodesh,* speaks through David and says:

> THE KINGS OF THE EARTH STAND UP, AND THE RULERS TAKE COUNSEL TOGETHER, AGAINST THE LORD, AND AGAINST HIS ANOINTED.

And in *Psalm* 2, verse 7, we have these words:

> I WILL TELL OF THE DECREE: THE LORD SAID UNTO ME: "THOU ART MY SON, THIS DAY HAVE I BEGOTTEN THEE."

Here is the Holy Spirit speaking through David and instructing him that the Lord, which is in Hebrew the ineffable name which we pronounce as *Adonai,* has a Son who is begotten of God in a supernatural way. Maybe King David himself did not understand the words that he was commanded to write by the Holy Spirit, but as Moses and Isaiah, he too obeyed. He wrote this down for us so there would be no misunderstanding. God who is almighty manifests Himself as a triunity, leaving us no doubt as to His nature.

But is such a concept Jewish? Is it not some Gentile or pagan concept that has somehow crept into our Holy Scriptures as some extreme liberalists would like to tell us? No, this was and still is a Jewish conception of God creating and dealing with His creation and His people Israel in a triune way. This quotation bears it out:

> *EXODUS* 19 STARTS WITH THE WORDS, "IN THE THIRD MONTH." THIS IS EXPLAINED BY THE WORDS OF *PROVERBS* 22:20, "HAVE I NOT WRITTEN UNTO THEE EXCELLENT (HEBREW, THREEFOLD) THINGS OF COUNSELS AND KNOWLEDGE." ON THIS RABBI JOSHUA BAR NEHEMIAH SAID THAT THIS IS THE TORAH* WHOSE LETTERS ARE THREEFOLD, *ALEPH, BET, GIML,* AND EVERYTHING IS A TRINITY: THE TORAH* IS TRINITARIAN, FOR IT IS COMPOSED OF THE TORAH,* THE PROPHETS, AND THE WRITINGS. THE MISHNA* (TALMUDICAL LEARNING) IS A TRINITY COMPOSED OF *TALMUD* (LEARNING), *HALACHOT* (DAILY JEWISH LAWS), AND *HAGGADOT* (HISTORICAL ITEMS). THE MEDIATOR CONSISTED OF A TRINITY OF MIRIAM, MOSES, AND AARON. PRAYERS ARE A TRINITY OF MORNING, AFTERNOON, AND EVENING PRAYERS. ISRAEL IS A TRINITY CONSISTING OF PRIESTS, LEVITES, AND ISRAELITES. THE NAME MOSES IN HEBREW CONSISTS OF THREE LETTERS. HE IS OF THE TRIBE OF LEVI, WHICH AGAIN IN HEBREW HAS THREE LETTERS; FROM THE SEED OF THE PATRIARCHS WHO ARE A TRINITY OF ABRAHAM, ISAAC, AND JACOB; IN THE THIRD MONTH WHICH IS *SIVAN*, AFTER *NISAN* AND *IYAR* ON MOUNT SIN WHOSE LETTERS ARE THREE AS IT IS WRITTEN, "AND THEY RESTED IN THE WILDERNESS OF SIN" (*Midrash Tanhuma* on *Exodus* 19).

If, according to our Rabbis, God has made everything and arranged everything in a trinitarian way, then it must be also Jewish and biblical to know that God Himself is a Trinity. This He is, and has manifested Himself as the Saviour-Messiah, the Son of God, in the person of Jesus. He then sent down the Holy Spirit, the *Ruach Hakodesh,* on the disciples in the third month, on the Feast of *Shavuot,* the feast of perfection, celebrated after counting seven times seven.

But can three be one? Does not common sense rebel against such a statement? Must we not state categorically that God is either One or Three? No so! As a matter of fact everything you come in contact with is not a mathematical concept of one, but usually an item composed of a trinity. Already the ancient Greek philosopher reasoned out the theory of atoms by watching a black cow, eating green grass, giving white milk. All things are composed of millions and billions of atoms; but the atom itself is a trinity of a proton, electron, and nucleus. Dr. Henry Heydt, in his commentary on *Romans* 1:20, says:

"Paul uses the creation of the kosmos as demonstrating this Godhead (theiotes). The universe (unus, one plus verterte, turn; turned into one, combined in one whole) is an absolute triunity of space, time, and matter. Each of these in turn is an absolute triunity. Space consists of length, breadth, and depth or height; time is future, present, and past; matter is energy, motion, and phenomena.

"Here we have not only an illustration of three in one—as in the case of light, heat, and ultra-violet rays of the sunbeam, or the manifestation of $H_2O$ as liquid, ice, and steam—but an absolute triunity composed of three absolute triunities."

We now have only to answer the question, "What does it all matter?" The answer is that it matters very much. It proves the truth of God's Word. The most important thing is what a Jewish follower of the Messiah Jesus said:

> FOR GOD SO LOVED THE WORLD THAT HE GAVE HIS ONLY BEGOTTEN SON THAT WHOSOEVER BELIEVETH IN HIM SHOULD NOT PERISH, BUT HAVE EVERLASTING LIFE (*John* 3:16).

Do you want to have peace in your heart and peace with your Creator? Accept this gift of God; confess your sins, and believe in the Messiah Jesus as the Korban* for your sins. Then you will have perfect peace.

> "BUT TO ALL WHO RECEIVED HIM, WHO BELIEVED IN HIS NAME, HE GAVE POWER TO BECOME CHILDREN OF GOD" (*John* 1:12).

# GLOSSARY

**Amoraim:** scholars active from completion of the Mishnah (c. 200 C. E.) until the completion of the Babylonian and Jerusalem Talmuds (end of the 4th and end of the 5th centuries).

**B.C.E.:** before the Common Era (B.C.)

**C.E.:** Common Era (A.D.)

**Gemara:** commentary and supplement to the Mishnah.

**Haftarah:** the selection from the Prophets read in the synagogue immediately after the reading of the Torah on Sabbaths and festivals.

**Ketuvim:** the Writings: Psalms, Proverbs, Job, Song of Songs, Ruth, Lamentations, Ecclesiastes, Esther, Daniel, Ezra, Nehemiah, and Chronicles.

**Korban:** sacrifice for guilt

**Masorah:** body of traditions regarding the correct spelling, writing, and reading of the Hebrew Bible.

**Menorah:** seven-branched candelabrum

**Midrash:** term meaning investigation or study applied to a special type of broad interpretation of the biblical text.

**Mishnah:** vast mass of oral interpretations and applications of the biblical law and decisions based thereon which accumulated from the days of Ezra (c. 450 B.C.E.) until the time of their final compilation about 200 C.E. by R. Judah Ha-Nasi.

**Nisan:** first month of the religious year, seventh month of secular calendar. Occurs in the spring. Passover begins on the 15th day of Nisan.

**Piyyut:** Hebrew compositions in poetical form which are included in the prayer book as additions to the established liturgy.

**Seder:** ceremony observed in the Jewish home on the first night of Passover, sometimes also the second night.

**Septuagint:** the Greek translation of Tenach made by 70 Jewish scholars (legend contained in the apocryphal Letter of Aristeas says 72 elders, six from each of the twelve tribes of Israel) in the first half of the third century B.C.E.

**Talmud:** collection of Jewish law and tradition, consisting of the Mishnah and the Gemara, and being either the edition produced in Palestine, called the Jerusalem Talmud, or the larger more important one produced in Babylon.

**Tanaim:** group of about 225 Jewish scholars active in Palestine for two and one half centuries after the death of Hillel. Recognized authorities on the Oral Law, their opinions being recorded in the Mishnah.

**Targum:** applied specifically to the Aramaic translation of various books of the Bible.

**Tenach:** name for the Bible, made up of three initials indicating its major sections: Torah (Pentateuch), Neviim (Prophets), and Ketuvim (Writings).

**Torah:** traditionally given to Moses at Sinai, and in a larger sense includes both the Written and the Oral Law, the entire Talmudic literature and commentaries. Also refers to the Five Books of Moses or the Pentateuch.

**Yom Kippur:** Day of Atonement

*OTHER LEDERER PUBLICATIONS*

The New Testament in Yiddish

The Good News According to Matthew

Yiddish Matthew

The Man with the Book

Would I? Would You?

Raisins and Almonds

The Ox, The Ass, The Oyster

The Messianic Passover Haggadah

It is Good! Growing up in a Messianic Jewish Family (a story coloring book)

The Most Famous Jew of All

To receive a free catalog or discuss issues in this book, call or write:

The Lederer Foundation
6204 Park Heights Avenue
Baltimore, MD 21215
(301) 358-6471